Study Guide & Working Papers

for

College Accounting

CHAPTERS 1-13

Thirteenth Edition

John Ellis Price, Ph.D., CPA
President and Professor of Accounting
University of North Texas at Dallas
Dallas, Texas

M. David Haddock, Jr., Ed.D., CPA
Professor of Accounting Emeritus
Chattanooga State Community College
Director of Training
Lattimore Black Morgan & Cain, PC
Brentwood, Tennessee

Michael J. Farina, MBA, CPA
Professor of Accounting
Cerritos College
Norwalk, California

The McGraw-Hill Companies

Study Guide & Working Papers for
COLLEGE ACCOUNTING, Thirteenth Edition
Chapters 1-13
John Ellis Price, M. David Haddock, Jr., and Michael J. Farina

Published by McGraw-Hill/Irwin, an imprint of The McGraw-Hill Companies, Inc., 1221 Avenue of the Americas, New York, NY 10020.

1 2 3 4 5 6 7 8 9 0 QDB/QDB 1 0 9 8 7 6 5 4 3 2 1

ISBN: 978-0-07-743057-3
MHID: 0-07-743057-3

www.mhhe.com

Table of Contents

Chapter 1	Accounting: The Language of Business	1
Chapter 2	Analyzing Business Transactions	5
Chapter 3	Analyzing Business Transactions Using T Accounts	21
Chapter 4	The General Journal and the General Ledger	41
Chapter 5	Adjustments and the Worksheet	73
Chapter 6	Closing Entries and the Postclosing Trial Balance	103
MINI-PRACTICE SET 1	Service Business Accounting Cycle	137
Chapter 7	Accounting for Sales and Accounts Receivable	151
Chapter 8	Accounting for Purchases and Accounts Payable	177
Chapter 9	Cash Receipts, Cash Payments, and Banking Procedures	207
Chapter 10	Payroll Computations, Records, and Payment	255
Chapter 11	Payroll Taxes, Deposits, and Reports	269
Chapter 12	Accruals, Deferrals, and the Worksheet	287
Chapter 13	Financial Statements and Closing Procedures	321
MINI-PRACTICE SET 2	Merchandising Business Accounting Cycle	365

CHAPTER 1

Accounting: The Language of Business

STUDY GUIDE

Understanding the Chapter

Objectives

1. Define accounting. **2.** Identify and discuss career opportunities in accounting. **3.** Identify the users of financial information. **4.** Compare and contrast the three types of business entities. **5.** Describe the process used to develop generally accepted accounting principles. **6.** Define the accounting terms new to this chapter.

Reading Assignment

Read Chapter 1 in the textbook. Complete the textbook Section Self Review as you finish reading each section of the chapter, and the Comprehensive Self Review at the end of the chapter. Refer to the Chapter 1 Glossary or to the Glossary at the end of the book to find definitions for terms that are not familiar to you.

Activities

- ❑ **Thinking Critically** — Answer the *Thinking Critically* questions for Google and Managerial Implications.
- ❑ **Discussion Questions** — Answer each assigned discussion question in Chapter 1.
- ❑ **Critical Thinking Problem** — Complete the critical thinking problem as assigned.
- ❑ **Business Connections** — Complete the Business Connections activities as assigned to gain a deeper understanding of Chapter 1 concepts.

Practice Tests

Complete the Practice Tests, which cover the main points in your reading assignment. Compare your answers with those in the Practice Test Answer Key for Chapter 1 at the end of this chapter. If you have answered any questions incorrectly, review the related section of the text.

Part A True-False *For each of the following statements, circle T in the answer column if the answer is true or F if the answer is false.*

T F 1. Passing a test called the Uniform CPA Examination is required for one to become a certified public accountant.

T F 2. The Securities and Exchange Commission has a great deal of power to dictate accounting methods used by companies whose stock is traded on the stock exchanges.

T F 3 The Securities and Exchange Commission often relies on pronouncements of the Financial Accounting Standards Board.

T F 4. The Financial Accounting Standards Board issues income tax rules.

T F 5. Because of the separate entity assumption, the personal financial activities of the owner of a sole proprietorship are combined with the financial affairs of his or her business in the accounting records of the business.

T F 6. All accounting principles are established by law.

T F 7. Because of the difference in the structures of the three types of business entities, certain aspects of their financial affairs are accounted for in different ways.

T F 8. A sole proprietorship is a form of business entity owned by two or more people.

T F 9. There is little difference between a corporation and other forms of business entities.

T F 10. Shares of stock represent ownership in a corporation.

T F 11. Employees should have no particular interest in the financial information about the business for which they work.

T F 12. The American Institute of Certified Public Accountants is a governmental agency.

T F 13. In a large company, the auditing process is completed by bookkeepers.

Part B Completion

In the answer column, supply the missing word or words needed to complete each of the following statements.

______ 1. The ______ and other tax authorities are interested in financial information about a firm.

______ 2. Corporate owners are called ______.

______ 3. Ownership in a corporation is evidenced by ______.

______ 4. The three major types of business entities are sole proprietorships, corporations, and ______.

______ 5. An economic entity is an organization whose major purpose is to produce a profit, whereas a(n) ______ is a nonprofit organization.

______ 6. The accounting process involves ______, ______, summarizing, interpreting, and communicating financial information about an economic or social entity.

______ 7. Periodic reports prepared from accounting records are called ______.

______ 8. Many people call accounting the ______ ______ ______.

______ 9. ______ is the study of accounting principles used by different countries.

______ 10. The IRS and the ______ have large numbers of accountants on their staff and use them to uncover possible violations of the law.

______ 11. Major areas of accounting are public accounting, managerial accounting, and ______.

______ 12. The ______ is an organization of accounting educators.

______ 13. The ______ is a national association of professional accountants.

______ 14. ______ are developed by the Financial Accounting Standards Board.

______ 15. The ______ was created to review and oversee the accounting methods of publicly owned corporations.

WORKING PAPERS

Name

CRITICAL THINKING PROBLEM 1.1

Chapter 1 Practice Test Answer Key

Part A True-False

1. T
2. T
3. T
4. F
5. F
6. F
7. T
8. F
9. F
10. T
11. F
12. F
13. F

Part B Completion

1. IRS
2. stockholders or shareholders
3. shares of stock
4. partnerships
5. social entity
6. recording, classifying
7. financial statements
8. language of business
9. International accounting
10. FBI
11. governmental accounting
12. AAA
13. AICPA
14. Generally accepted accounting principles
15. SEC

CHAPTER 2

Analyzing Business Transactions

STUDY GUIDE

STUDY GUIDE

Understanding the Chapter

Objectives

1. Record in equation form the financial effects of a business transaction. **2.** Define, identify, and understand the relationship between asset, liability, and owner's equity accounts. **3.** Analyze the effects of business transactions on a firm's assets, liabilities, and owner's equity and record these effects in accounting equation form. **4.** Prepare an income statement. **5.** Prepare a statement of owner's equity and a balance sheet **6.** Define the accounting terms new to this chapter.

Reading Assignment

Read Chapter 2 in the textbook. Complete the textbook Section Self Review as you finish reading each section of the chapter, and the Comprehensive Self Review at the end of the chapter. Refer to the Chapter 2 Glossary or to the Glossary at the end of the book to find definitions for terms that are not familiar to you.

Activities

❑ **Thinking Critically** — Answer the *Thinking Critically* questions for Southwest Airlines and Managerial Implications.

❑ **Discussion Questions** — Answer each assigned discussion question in Chapter 2.

❑ **Exercises** — Complete each assigned exercise in Chapter 2. Use the forms provided in this SGWP. The objectives covered by an exercise are given after the exercise number. If you need help with an exercise, review the portion of the chapter related to the objective(s) covered.

❑ **Problems A/B** — Complete each assigned problem in Chapter 2. Use the forms provided in this SGWP. The objectives covered by a problem are given after the problem number. If you need help with a problem, review the portion of the chapter related to the objective(s) covered.

❑ **Critical Thinking Problems 2.1 and 2.2** — Complete Critical Thinking Problems 2.1 and 2.2 as assigned. Use the forms provided in this SGWP.

❑ **Business Connections** — Complete the Business Connections activities as assigned to gain a deeper understanding of Chapter 2 concepts.

Practice Tests

Complete the Practice Tests, which cover the main points in your reading assignment. Compare your answers with those in the Practice Test Answer Key for Chapter 2 at the end of this chapter. If you have answered any questions incorrectly, review the related section of the text.

Part A True-False *For each of the following statements, circle T in the answer column if the answer is true or F if the answer is false.*

T F **1.** When equipment is purchased for cash, there is no change in the total value of the firm's property.

T F **2.** The balance sheet is prepared at the end of the accounting period to show the results of operations.

T F **3.** A net loss results if total expenses exceed total revenue.

T F **4** Profit and loss statement is another name for the income statement.

T F **5.** The balance sheet shows the financial position of a business on a specific date.

T F **6.** The net income or net loss for the period is shown in the Assets section of the balance sheet.

T F **7.** The net income or net loss for the period is shown on both the income statement and the statement of owner's equity.

T F **8.** The collection of cash from accounts receivable increases owner's equity.

T F **9.** Expenses decrease owner's equity.

T F **10.** Revenue decreases owner's equity.

Part B Matching *For each numbered item, choose the matching term from the box and write the identifying letter in the answer column.*

______ **1.** Amounts owed by charge account customers.

______ **2.** Amount remaining when total revenue is more than total expenses.

______ **3.** Those to whom money is owed.

______ **4.** Owner's financial interest in the business.

______ **5.** Property owned by a business.

______ **6.** A business obligation or debt.

______ **7.** An expression of the relationship in which assets equal liabilities plus owner's equity.

______ **8.** Inflows of money or other assets resulting from sales of goods or service.

a. Accounts Receivable
b. Assets
c. Creditors
d. Revenue
e. Owner's equity
f. Liability
g. Net income
h. Fundamental accounting equation

Part C Completion *In the answer column, supply the missing word or words needed to complete each of the following statements.*

______ **1.** Accountants must ______ each business transaction before they can intelligently record, report, and interpret it.

______ **2.** The purchase of new equipment on account creates a debt that is called a(n) ______.

______ **3.** When property values and financial interest increase or decrease, the sum of the items on both sides of the equation always remains ______.

______ **4.** The basic reason for starting a business is the possibility of making a ______.

______ **5.** Accounts receivable result when goods are sold or services are performed on ______.

______ **6.** When expenses are paid, the owner's equity is ______.

______ **7.** Regardless of the number and variety of transactions, liabilities plus owner's equity always equal ______.

______ **8.** When supplies are first purchased for use in operations, they are considered a type of ______.

Demonstration Problem

The account balances for Thomas Neal, CPA, for the month of January 2013 are shown below in random order.

Rent Expense	$ 8,000	Advertising Expense	$ 5,000
Fees Earned	138,240	Office Equipment	51,120
Accounts Payable	29,824	T. Neal, Drawing	15,156
Salaries Expense	23,780	Accounts Receivable	29,800
Cash	182,276	T. Neal, Capital 1/1	?

Instructions

1. Determine the balance for **Thomas Neal, Capital,** on January 1, 2013.
2. Prepare an income statement, a statement of owner's equity, and a balance sheet as of January 31, 2013.
3. List the expenses on the income statement in alphabetical order.

SOLUTION

Determine the balance for Thomas Neal Capital, on January 1, 2013.
Let Thomas Neal, Capital = X. Solving for X:

		Assets			=	Liabilities +		Owner's Equity				
Cash	+	Accts. Rec.	+	Office Equip.	=	Accounts Payable	+	T. Neal, Capital	− Drawing	+ Revenue	−	Expenses
182,276	+	29,800	+	51,120	=	29,824	+	X	− 15,156	+ 138,240	−	36,780
				263,196	=	116,128	+	X				
		263,196	−	116,128	=	116,128	−	116,128 +	X			
				116,128	=	X						

Thomas Neal, Capital, January 1, 2013 = **$147,068**

Total Expenses:

Rent Expense	$ 8,000
Salaries Expense	23,780
Advertising Expense	5,000
	$36,780

Thomas Neal, CPA
Income Statement
Month Ended January 31, 2013

Revenue		
Fees Earned		138 240 00
Expenses		
Rent Expense	8 000 00	
Salaries Expense	23 780 00	
Advertising Expense	5 000 00	
Total Expenses		36 780 00
Net Income		101 460 00

Thomas Neal, CPA
Statement of Owner's Equity
Month Ended January 31, 2013

Thomas Neal, Capital, January 1, 2013		147 068 00
Net Income	101 460 00	
Less Withdrawals	15 156 00	
Increase in Capital		86 304 00
Thomas Neal, Capital, January 31, 2013		233 372 00

SOLUTION (continued)

Thomas Neal, CPA

Balance Sheet

January 31, 2013

Assets		Liabilities	
Cash	182 2 7 6 00	Accounts Payable	29 8 2 4 00
Accounts Receivable	29 8 0 0 00	Owner's Equity	
Office Equipment	51 1 2 0 00	Thomas Neal, Capital	233 3 7 2 00
Total Assets	263 1 9 6 00	Total Liabilities and Owner's Equity	263 1 9 6 00

WORKING PAPERS

Name ______________________

EXERCISE 2.1

Assets ______________________

Liabilities ______________________

Owner's Equity ______________________

EXERCISE 2.2

1. ______________________

2. ______________________

3. ______________________

4. ______________________

5. ______________________

EXERCISE 2.3

	Assets	=	Liabilities	+	Owner's Equity
1.		=		+	
2.		=		+	
3.		=		+	
4.		=		+	
5.		=		+	

EXERCISE 2.4

Transaction	Assets	=	Liabilities	+	Owner's Equity
1.	+	=		+	+
2.		=		+	
3.		=		+	
4.		=		+	
5.		=		+	

Name ____________________

EXERCISE 2.5

	Assets			=	Liabilities +	Owner's Equity		
	Cash	+ Accounts Receivable	+ Equipment	=	Accounts Payable	+ Amos Roberts Capital	+ Revenue	− Expenses
1.								
2.								
3.								
4.								
5.								
6.								
7.								
8.								
Totals		+	+	=		+	+	−

EXERCISE 2.6

Revenue

Expenses

EXERCISE 2.7

1.
2.
3.
4.
5.
6.
7.

Name

EXERCISE 2.8

EXERCISE 2.9

Revenue

Expenses

Name

EXERCISE 2.10

Name

PROBLEM 2.1A or 2.1B

	Assets							=	Liabilities	+	Owner's Equity
	Cash	+	Accounts Receivable	+	Supplies	+	Equipment	=	Accounts Payable	+	Owner's Capital
1.											
2.											
3.											
4.											
5.											
6.											
7.											
8.											
9.											
10.											
11.											
Totals		+		+		+		=		+	

Analyze:

Name ____________________

PROBLEM 2.2A or 2.2B

	Assets				= Liabilities +	Owner's Equity		
	Cash	+ Accounts Receivable	+	+	= Accounts Payable	+ Capital	+ Revenue	− Expenses
Beginning Balances		+	+	+	=	+	+	−
1.								
New Balances		+	+	+	=	+	+	−
2.								
New Balances		+	+	+	=	+	+	−
3.								
New Balances		+	+	+	=	+	+	−
4.								
New Balances		+	+	+	=	+	+	−
5.								
New Balances		+	+	+	=	+	+	−
6.								
New Balances		+	+	+	=	+	+	−
7.								
New Balances		+	+	+	=	+	+	−
8.								
New Balances		+	+	+	=	+	+	−
9.								
New Balances		+	+	+	=	+	+	−
10.								
New Balances		+	+	+	=	+	+	−

Analyze: ____________________

Name

PROBLEM 2.3A or 2.3B

Analyze:

PROBLEM 2.4A or 2.4B

Name

PROBLEM 2.4A or 2.4B (continued)

Analyze:

Name

CRITICAL THINKING PROBLEM 2.1

Name ______________________

CRITICAL THINKING PROBLEM 2.2

Determine the balance for **Dolly Garcia**, April 30, 2013.

Assets			= Liabilities +	Owner's Equity			
Cash	+ Accounts Receivable	+ Machinery	= Accounts Payable	+ D. Garcia Capital	− D. Garcia Drawing	+ Revenue	− Expenses
$26,000	+ $10,800	+ $19,000	= $12,800	+ ?	− $5,200	+ $23,800	− $17,150

Let Dolly Garcia, Capital = X.

Solving for X:

Dolly Garcia, Capital, April 1, 2013,= ______

Advertising Expense	$ 3,750
Maintenance Expense	4,400
Salaries Expense	9,000
Total Expenses	

Name

CRITICAL THINKING PROBLEM 2.2 (continued)

Analyze:

Chapter 2 Practice Test Answer Key

Part A True-False

1. T	6. F
2. F	7. T
3. T	8. F
4. T	9. T
5. T	10. F

Part B Matching

1. a	5. b
2. g	6. f
3. c	7. h
4. e	8. d

Part C Completion

1. analyze
2. accounts payable or liability
3. equal
4. profit
5. credit or on account
6. reduced or decreased
7. assets
8. asset or property

CHAPTER 3

Analyzing Business Transactions Using T Accounts

STUDY GUIDE

Understanding the Chapter

Objectives

1. Set up T accounts for assets, liabilities, and owner's equity. **2.** Analyze business transactions and enter them in the accounts. **3.** Determine the balance of an account. **4.** Set up T accounts for revenue and expenses. **5.** Prepare a trial balance from T accounts. **6.** Prepare an income statement, a statement of owner's equity, and a balance sheet. **7.** Develop a chart of accounts. **8.** Define the accounting terms new to this chapter.

Reading Assignment

Read Chapter 3 in the textbook. Complete the textbook Section Self Review as you finish reading each section of the chapter, and the Comprehensive Self Review at the end of the chapter. Refer to the Chapter 3 Glossary or to the Glossary at the end of the book to find definitions for terms that are not familiar to you.

Activities

- ❑ **Thinking Critically** — Answer the *Thinking Critically* questions for AT&T and Managerial Implications.
- ❑ **Discussion Questions** — Answer each assigned discussion question in Chapter 3.
- ❑ **Exercises** — Complete each assigned exercise in Chapter 3. Use the forms provided in this SGWP. The objectives covered by an exercise are given after the exercise number. If you need help with an exercise, review the portion of the chapter related to the objective(s) covered.
- ❑ **Problems A/B** — Complete each assigned problem in Chapter 3. Use the forms provided in this SGWP. The objectives covered by a problem are given after the problem number. If you need help with a problem, review the portion of the chapter related to the objective(s) covered.
- ❑ **Critical Thinking Problems** — Complete the critical thinking problems as assigned. Use the forms provided in this SGWP.
- ❑ **Business Connections** — Complete the Business Connections activities as assigned to gain a deeper understanding of Chapter 3 concepts.

Practice Tests

Complete the Practice Tests, which cover the main points in your reading assignment. Compare your answers with those in the Practice Test Answer Key for Chapter 3 at the end of this chapter. If you have answered any questions incorrectly, review the related section of the text.

Part A True-False *For each of the following statements, circle T in the answer column if the answer is true or F if the answer is false.*

T F 1. The **Accounts Payable** account is decreased by a debit entry.

T F 2. Increases in expense accounts are recorded by credit entries.

T F 3. Accountants keep a separate record for each asset, liability, and owner's equity item.

T F 4. The T account allows increases and decreases to be separated and recorded on different sides.

T F 5. Increases in assets are recorded on the debit side of an account.

T F 6. Decreases in assets are recorded on the left side of an account.

T F 7. The owner's beginning investment is entered as a debit in the owner's capital account.

T F 8. Increases in liabilities are recorded on the debit side of an account.

T F 9. A cash payment by a business is recorded as a debit entry in the **Cash** account.

T F 10. Decreases in liabilities are credited to the liability account.

T F 11. An increase in the owner's investment is recorded by crediting the owner's capital account.

T F 12. Revenue accounts are increased by credits.

T F 13. An entry on the left side of any account is called a debit.

T F 14. A reduction in the equity of the owners is recorded by making a debit entry in the **Owner's Drawing** account.

T F 15. The receipt of cash is recorded by a debit entry to the **Cash** account.

Part B Matching

For each numbered item, choose the matching item from the box and write the identifying letter in the answer column.

a. Account
b. Double-entry system
c. Credit
d. Permanent accounts
e. Temporary accounts
f. Expense
g. Revenue
h. Chart of accounts
i. Debit

_______ **1.** An operating cost that decreases owner's equity.

_______ **2.** The system of accounting that requires equality of the entries on each side of the equation.

_______ **3.** Accounts whose balances are carried forward to start a new period.

_______ **4.** An entry on the left side of an account.

_______ **5.** An entry on the right side of an account.

_______ **6.** A system for arranging accounts in logical order.

_______ **7.** Accounts whose balances are transferred to a summary account at the end of the accounting period.

_______ **8.** A subdivision of owner's equity that is used to record various types of income of a business.

_______ **9.** A separate written record that is kept for each asset, liability, and owner's equity item.

Part C Completion

In the answer column, supply the missing word or words needed to complete each of the following statements.

_______________ **1.** The ______ of an account is where increases in the account are recorded and where the balance is recorded.

_______________ **2.** The ______ is a statement prepared to test the accuracy of the figures recorded in the accounts.

_______________ **3.** A(n) ______ is an error where the digits of a number are switched.

_______________ **4.** A(n) ______ is an error where the decimal point is misplaced.

_______________ **5.** A(n) ______ is the total of several entries on either side of an account that is entered in small pencil.

Demonstration Problem

Nina Turner is an investment broker who operates her own business, Turner Investment Counseling.

Instructions

1. Analyze the transactions for the month of January 2013, and record each in the appropriate T accounts. Use plus and minus signs to show increases and decreases. Identify each entry in the T accounts by writing the number of the transaction next to the entry.
2. Determine the balance for each T account. Prepare a trial balance.

Transactions

1. Nina Turner invested $50,000 in cash to start the business.
2. Turner Investment Counseling purchased office furniture for $9,000 on account.
3. Paid $3,000 for one month's rent.
4. Sold an investment portfolio to the Dotson Family and received fees of $50,000.
5. Purchased a computer for $4,000, paying $2,000 in cash and putting the balance on account for 60 days.
6. Paid $8,400 for employee salaries.
7. Purchased office equipment for $7,500 with credit terms of 60 days.
8. Sold an investment portfolio to the Carter Family and will receive commission fees of $21,000 in 30 days.
9. Issued a check for $3,750 for partial payment of the amount for office equipment.
10. Nina Turner withdrew $5,000 in cash for personal use.
11. Issued a check for $1,040 to pay the utility bill.

SOLUTION

Cash

	Debit		Credit
(1)	+ 50,000	(3)	– 3,000
(4)	+ 50,000	(5)	– 2,000
		(6)	– 8,400
		(9)	– 3,750
	100,000	(10)	– 5,000
		(11)	– 1,040
Bal.	76,810		23,190

Accounts Receivable

	Debit		Credit
(8)	+ 21,000		

Office Furniture

	Debit		Credit
(2)	+ 9,000		

Office Equipment

	Debit		Credit
(5)	+ 4,000		
(7)	+ 7,500		
Bal.	11,500		

Accounts Payable

	Debit		Credit
(9)	– 3,750	(2)	+ 9,000
		(5)	+ 2,000
		(7)	+ 7,500
		Bal.	14,750

Nina Turner, Capital

	Debit		Credit
		(1)	+ 50,000

Nina Turner, Drawing

	Debit		Credit
(10)	+ 5,000		

Fees Income

	Debit		Credit
		(4)	+ 50,000
		(8)	+ 21,000
		Bal.	71,000

Rent Expense

	Debit		Credit
(3)	+ 3,000		

Salaries Expense

	Debit		Credit
(6)	+ 8,400		

Utilities Expense

	Debit		Credit
(11)	+ 1040		

SOLUTION (continued)

Turner Investment Counseling

Trial Balance

January 31, 2013

ACCOUNT NAME	DEBIT	CREDIT
Cash	76 8 1 0 00	
Accounts Receivable	2 1 0 0 0 00	
Office Furniture	9 0 0 0 00	
Office Equipment	11 5 0 0 00	
Accounts Payable		14 7 5 0 00
Nina Turner, Capital		50 0 0 0 00
Nina Turner, Drawing	5 0 0 0 00	
Fees Income		71 0 0 0 00
Rent Expense	3 0 0 0 00	
Salaries Expense	8 4 0 0 00	
Utilities Expense	1 0 4 0 00	
Totals	135 7 5 0 00	135 7 5 0 00

WORKING PAPERS

Name ______________________________

EXERCISE 3.1

EXERCISE 3.2

EXERCISE 3.3

1. ______________________________
2. ______________________________
3. ______________________________
4. ______________________________
5. ______________________________
6. ______________________________
7. ______________________________
8. ______________________________

Name

EXERCISE 3.4

1.
2.
3.
4.
5.

EXERCISE 3.5

EXERCISE 3.6

ACCOUNT NAME	DEBIT	CREDIT

Name

EXERCISE 3.6 (continued)

EXERCISE 3.7

Name

EXERCISE 3.7 (continued)

EXERCISE 3.8

Name

PROBLEM 3.1A or 3.1B

1.

2.

3.

4.

5.

6.

7.

8.

Analyze:

PROBLEM 3.2A or 3.2B

1.

2.

3.

4.

5.

6.

7.

8.

Analyze:

Name

PROBLEM 3.3A or 3.3B

1.

2.

3.

4.

5.

6.

7.

8.

9.

10.

11.

12.

Name ______________________

PROBLEM 3.4A or 3.4B

Analyze: ______________________

Name

PROBLEM 3.5A or 3.5B

ACCOUNT NAME	DEBIT	CREDIT

Name

PROBLEM 3.5A or 3.5B (continued)

Analyze:

Name

CRITICAL THINKING PROBLEM 3.1

Name

CRITICAL THINKING PROBLEM 3.1 (continued)

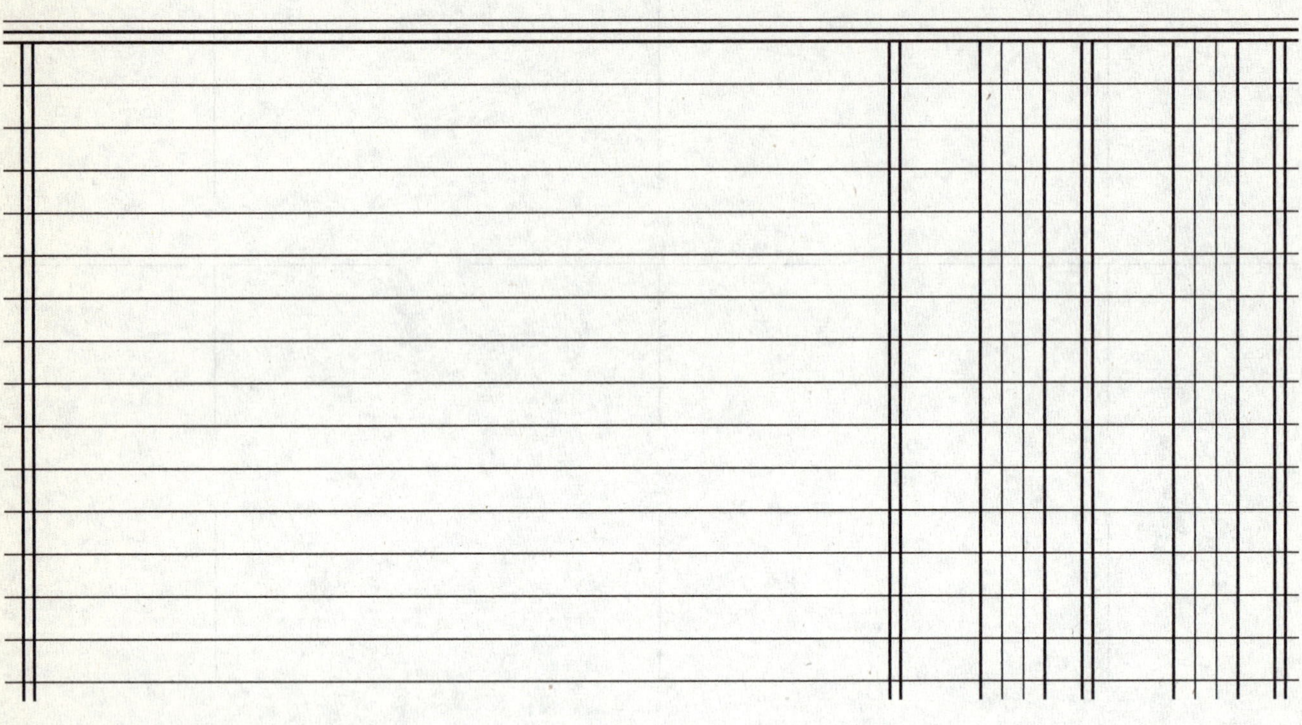

Name

CRITICAL THINKING PROBLEM 3.1 (continued)

Name

CRITICAL THINKING PROBLEM 3.2

Name

CRITICAL THINKING PROBLEM 3.2 (continued)

ACCOUNT NAME	DEBIT	CREDIT

Name

CRITICAL THINKING PROBLEM 3.2 (continued)

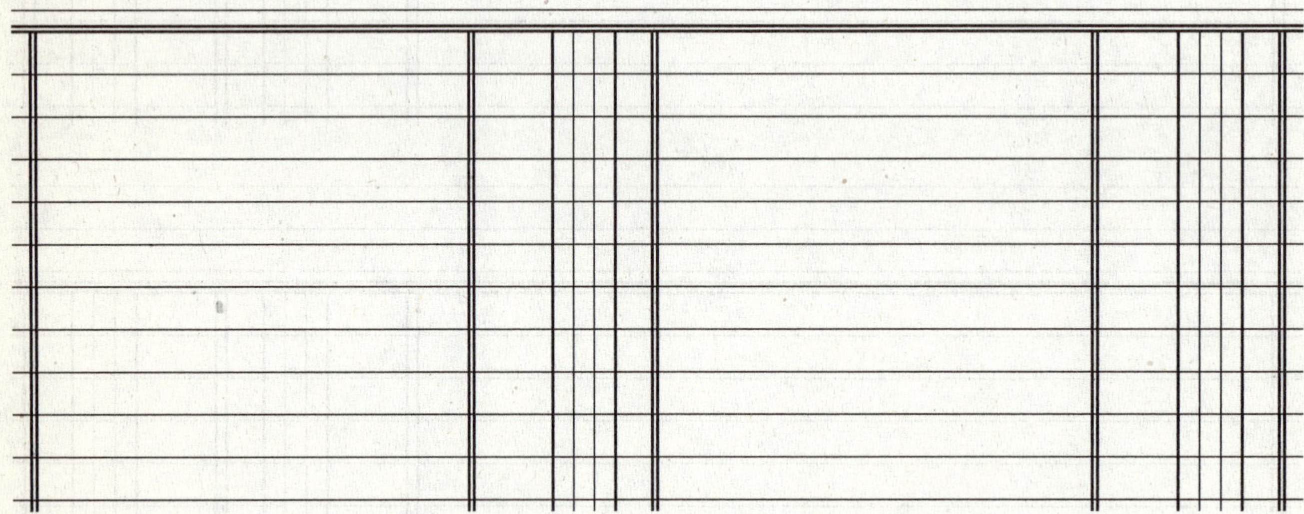

Analyze:

Chapter 3 Practice Test Answer Key

Part A True-False

1. T	6. F	11. T
2. F	7. F	12. T
3. T	8. F	13. T
4. T	9. F	14. T
5. T	10. F	15. T

Part B Matching

1. f	6. h
2. b	7. e
3. d	8. g
4. i	9. a
5. c	

Part C Completion

1. normal balance
2. trial balance
3. transposition
4. slide
5. footing

CHAPTER 4 The General Journal and the General Ledger

STUDY GUIDE

Understanding the Chapter

Objectives

1. Record transactions in the general journal. **2.** Prepare compound journal entries. **3.** Post journal entries to general ledger accounts. **4.** Correct errors made in the journal or ledger. **5.** Define the accounting terms new to this chapter.

Reading Assignment

Read Chapter 4 in the textbook. Complete the textbook Section Self Review as you finish reading each section of the chapter, and the Comprehensive Self Review at the end of the chapter. Refer to the Chapter 4 Glossary or to the Glossary at the end of the book to find definitions for terms that are not familiar to you.

Activities

- ❑ **Thinking Critically** — Answer the *Thinking Critically* questions for Willamette Valley Vineyards and Managerial Implications.
- ❑ **Discussion Questions** — Answer each assigned discussion question in Chapter 4.
- ❑ **Exercises** — Complete each assigned exercise in Chapter 4. Use the forms provided in this SGWP. The objectives covered by an exercise are given after the exercise number. If you need help with an exercise, review the portion of the chapter related to the objective(s) covered.
- ❑ **Problems A/B** — Complete each assigned problem in Chapter 4. Use the forms provided in this SGWP. The objectives covered by a problem are given after the problem number. If you need help with a problem, review the portion of the chapter related to the objective(s) covered.
- ❑ **Critical Thinking Problems** — Complete the critical thinking problems as assigned. Use the forms provided in this SGWP.
- ❑ **Business Connections** — Complete the Business Connections activities as assigned to gain a deeper understanding of Chapter 4 concepts.

Practice Tests

Complete the Practice Tests, which cover the main points in your reading assignment. Compare your answers with those in the Practice Test Answer Key for Chapter 4 at the end of this chapter. If you have answered any questions incorrectly, review the related section of the text.

Part A Matching *For each numbered item, choose the matching term from the box and write the identifying letter in the answer column.*

a. journal
b. source documents
c. posting
d. general ledger
e. T accounts
f. journalizing
g. correcting entry
h. compound entry
i. balance ledger form
j. audit trail

_______ **1.** A ledger account form that always shows the current balance of an account.

_______ **2.** A journal entry that consists of more than one debit or more than one credit.

_______ **3.** A permanent, classified record of all accounts used by a business.

_______ **4.** Used to analyze transactions but not used to maintain financial records.

_______ **5.** The process of transferring information from the journal to the ledger.

_______ **6.** An entry that is made when there is an error in data that has been journalized and posted.

_______ **7.** Record of original entry.

_______ **8.** The process of recording transactions in the journal.

_______ **9.** Invoices and other business forms that contain the original data about transactions.

_______ **10.** A chain of references that makes it possible to trace information about transactions through an accounting system.

Part B Completion *In the answer column, supply the missing word or words needed to complete each of the following statements.*

_______________ **1.** The accountant always records the ______ items first in the Description column of the journal.

_______________ **2.** The ______ is always entered at the top of the Date column.

_______________ **3.** The accountant enters transactions in the general journal in ______ order.

_______________ **4.** The pages in the ledger are usually organized so that the ______ come first.

_______________ **5.** If an error is discovered in a journal before the entry is ______, the error can be neatly crossed out and the correct data written above it.

_______________ **6.** All the accounts together constitute a(n) ______, or a record of final entry.

_______________ **7.** Notations that allow the data in journals and ledgers to be easily traced are called ______.

_______________ **8.** Descriptions in the general journal should be complete but ______.

_______________ **9.** On the balance ledger form the second money column is used to record ______ amounts.

_______________ **10.** On the balance ledger form the first money column is used to record ______ amounts.

Demonstration Problem

On January 1, 2013, John Wilson opened his consulting office and began business as Wilson Consulting Services. Selected transactions for the first month of operations follow.

Instructions

1. Journalize the transactions on page 1 of a general journal. Write the year at the top of the Date column; include an explanation for each entry.
2. Post to the general ledger accounts.
3. Prepare a trial balance.

DATE	TRANSACTIONS
January 1	John Wilson invested $90,000 cash in the business.
2	Issued Check 101 for $5,000 to pay the January rent.
5	Purchased office equipment for $30,000 from Davis Office Supply, Invoice 7045; issued Check 102 for $10,000 down payment with the balance due in 30 days.
12	Wrote a lease contract for Ned Lee for $6,000 cash.
15	Performed consulting services for a client, Jones Supply Company, for $20,000 to be received in 30 days.
28	Issued Check 103 for $10,000 for payment to Davis Office Supply.
29	Issued Check 104 for $10,000 to John Wilson for personal use.
31	Received $9,000 from Jones Supply Company for partial payment of their account.

SOLUTION

GENERAL JOURNAL

PAGE 1

DATE		DESCRIPTION	POST. REF.	DEBIT	CREDIT
2013					
Jan.	1	Cash	101	90,000.00	
		John Wilson, Capital	301		90,000.00
		Investment to start business			
	2	Rent Expense	514	5,000.00	
		Cash	101		5,000.00
		Issued Check 101 for January rent			
	5	Office Equipment	131	30,000.00	
		Cash	101		10,000.00
		Accounts Payable	202		20,000.00
		Issued Check 102 for office equipment,			
		balance due in 30 days.			
	12	Cash	101	6,000.00	
		Fees Income	401		6,000.00
		Performed services for cash.			
	15	Accounts Receivable	111	20,000.00	
		Fees Income	401		20,000.00
		Performed services on account.			
	28	Accounts Payable	202	10,000.00	
		Cash	101		10,000.00
		Paid Invoice 7045, Check 103			
	29	John Wilson, Drawing	302	10,000.00	
		Cash	101		10,000.00
		Issued Check 104 to owner for personal use.			
	31	Cash	101	9,000.00	
		Accounts Receivable	111		9,000.00
		Received partial payment			
		from Jones Supply Company			

SOLUTION (continued)

GENERAL LEDGER

ACCOUNT Cash — ACCOUNT NO. 101

DATE		DESCRIPTION	POST. REF.	DEBIT	CREDIT	BALANCE DEBIT	BALANCE CREDIT
2013							
Jan.	1		J1	90 0 0 0 00		90 0 0 0 00	
	2		J1		5 0 0 0 00	85 0 0 0 00	
	5		J1		10 0 0 0 00	75 0 0 0 00	
	12		J1	6 0 0 0 00		81 0 0 0 00	
	28		J1		10 0 0 0 00	71 0 0 0 00	
	29		J1		10 0 0 0 00	61 0 0 0 00	
	31		J1	9 0 0 0 00		70 0 0 0 00	

ACCOUNT Accounts Receivable — ACCOUNT NO. 111

DATE		DESCRIPTION	POST. REF.	DEBIT	CREDIT	BALANCE DEBIT	BALANCE CREDIT
2013							
Jan.	15		J1	20 0 0 0 00		20 0 0 0 00	
	31		J1		9 0 0 0 00	11 0 0 0 00	

ACCOUNT Office Equipment — ACCOUNT NO. 131

DATE		DESCRIPTION	POST. REF.	DEBIT	CREDIT	BALANCE DEBIT	BALANCE CREDIT
2013							
Jan.	5		J1	30 0 0 0 00		30 0 0 0 00	

ACCOUNT Accounts Payable — ACCOUNT NO. 202

DATE		DESCRIPTION	POST. REF.	DEBIT	CREDIT	BALANCE DEBIT	BALANCE CREDIT
2013							
Jan.	5		J1		20 0 0 0 00		20 0 0 0 00
	28		J1	10 0 0 0 00			10 0 0 0 00

ACCOUNT John Wilson, Capital — ACCOUNT NO. 301

DATE		DESCRIPTION	POST. REF.	DEBIT	CREDIT	BALANCE DEBIT	BALANCE CREDIT
2013							
Jan.	1		J1		90 0 0 0 00		90 0 0 0 00

SOLUTION (continued)

ACCOUNT **John Wilson, Drawing** ACCOUNT NO. **302**

DATE		DESCRIPTION	POST. REF.	DEBIT	CREDIT	BALANCE DEBIT	BALANCE CREDIT
2013							
Jan.	**29**		**J1**	**10,000.00**		**10,000.00**	

ACCOUNT **Fees Income** ACCOUNT NO. **401**

DATE		DESCRIPTION	POST. REF.	DEBIT	CREDIT	BALANCE DEBIT	BALANCE CREDIT
2013							
Jan.	**12**		**J1**		**6,000.00**		**6,000.00**
	15		**J1**		**20,000.00**		**26,000.00**

ACCOUNT **Rent Expense** ACCOUNT NO. **514**

DATE		DESCRIPTION	POST. REF.	DEBIT	CREDIT	BALANCE DEBIT	BALANCE CREDIT
2013							
Jan.	**2**		**J1**	**5,000.00**		**5,000.00**	

Wilson Consulting Services

Trial Balance

January 31, 2013

ACCOUNT NAME	DEBIT	CREDIT
Cash	**70,000.00**	
Accounts Receivable	**11,000.00**	
Office Equipment	**30,000.00**	
Accounts Payable		**10,000.00**
John Wilson, Capital		**90,000.00**
John Wilson, Drawing	**10,000.00**	
Fees Income		**26,000.00**
Rent Expense	**5,000.00**	
Totals	**126,000.00**	**126,000.00**

WORKING PAPERS

Name ______________________

EXERCISE 4.1

	Debit	Credit		Debit	Credit		Debit	Credit
1.			5.			8.		
2.			6.			9.		
3.			7.			10.		
4.								

EXERCISE 4.2

GENERAL JOURNAL

PAGE ______

	DATE		DESCRIPTION	POST. REF.	DEBIT	CREDIT	
1							1
2							2
3							3
4							4
5							5
6							6
7							7
8							8
9							9
10							10
11							11
12							12
13							13
14							14
15							15
16							16
17							17
18							18
19							19
20							20
21							21
22							22
23							23
24							24
25							25
26							26
27							27
28							28
29							29

Name ______________________

EXERCISE 4.2 (continued)

GENERAL JOURNAL PAGE ______

DATE		DESCRIPTION	POST. REF.	DEBIT	CREDIT

EXERCISE 4.3

GENERAL LEDGER

ACCOUNT ______________________ ACCOUNT NO. ______

DATE		DESCRIPTION	POST. REF.	DEBIT	CREDIT	BALANCE	
						DEBIT	CREDIT

Name

EXERCISE 4.3 (continued)

GENERAL LEDGER

ACCOUNT ______________________ ACCOUNT NO. ______

DATE		DESCRIPTION	POST. REF.	DEBIT	CREDIT	BALANCE	
						DEBIT	CREDIT

ACCOUNT ______________________ ACCOUNT NO. ______

DATE		DESCRIPTION	POST. REF.	DEBIT	CREDIT	BALANCE	
						DEBIT	CREDIT

ACCOUNT ______________________ ACCOUNT NO. ______

DATE		DESCRIPTION	POST. REF.	DEBIT	CREDIT	BALANCE	
						DEBIT	CREDIT

ACCOUNT ______________________ ACCOUNT NO. ______

DATE		DESCRIPTION	POST. REF.	DEBIT	CREDIT	BALANCE	
						DEBIT	CREDIT

ACCOUNT ______________________ ACCOUNT NO. ______

DATE		DESCRIPTION	POST. REF.	DEBIT	CREDIT	BALANCE	
						DEBIT	CREDIT

Name ______________________

EXERCISE 4.3 (continued)

GENERAL LEDGER

ACCOUNT ______________________ ACCOUNT NO. ________

DATE		DESCRIPTION	POST. REF.	DEBIT	CREDIT	BALANCE DEBIT	BALANCE CREDIT

ACCOUNT ______________________ ACCOUNT NO. ________

DATE		DESCRIPTION	POST. REF.	DEBIT	CREDIT	BALANCE DEBIT	BALANCE CREDIT

ACCOUNT ______________________ ACCOUNT NO. ________

DATE		DESCRIPTION	POST. REF.	DEBIT	CREDIT	BALANCE DEBIT	BALANCE CREDIT

ACCOUNT ______________________ ACCOUNT NO. ________

DATE		DESCRIPTION	POST. REF.	DEBIT	CREDIT	BALANCE DEBIT	BALANCE CREDIT

ACCOUNT ______________________ ACCOUNT NO. ________

DATE		DESCRIPTION	POST. REF.	DEBIT	CREDIT	BALANCE DEBIT	BALANCE CREDIT

ACCOUNT ______________________ ACCOUNT NO. ________

DATE		DESCRIPTION	POST. REF.	DEBIT	CREDIT	BALANCE DEBIT	BALANCE CREDIT

Name

EXERCISE 4.4

GENERAL JOURNAL

PAGE

DATE	DESCRIPTION	POST. REF.	DEBIT	CREDIT

Name ____________________

EXERCISE 4.5

GENERAL JOURNAL PAGE ______

	DATE		DESCRIPTION	POST. REF.	DEBIT	CREDIT	
1							1
2							2
3							3
4							4
5							5
6							6

EXERCISE 4.6

GENERAL JOURNAL PAGE ______

	DATE		DESCRIPTION	POST. REF.	DEBIT	CREDIT	
1							1
2							2
3							3
4							4
5							5
6							6

EXTRA FORM

GENERAL JOURNAL PAGE ______

	DATE		DESCRIPTION	POST. REF.	DEBIT	CREDIT	
1							1
2							2
3							3
4							4
5							5
6							6
7							7
8							8
9							9
10							10
11							11
12							12
13							13

Name

PROBLEM 4.1A or 4.1B

GENERAL JOURNAL

PAGE

DATE		DESCRIPTION	POST. REF.	DEBIT	CREDIT

Name

PROBLEM 4.1A or 4.1B (continued)

GENERAL JOURNAL

PAGE

DATE	DESCRIPTION	POST. REF.	DEBIT	CREDIT

Analyze:

Name

PROBLEM 4.2A or 4.2B

GENERAL JOURNAL

PAGE

DATE	DESCRIPTION	POST. REF.	DEBIT	CREDIT

Name

PROBLEM 4.2A or 4.2B (continued)

GENERAL JOURNAL

PAGE

DATE	DESCRIPTION	POST. REF.	DEBIT	CREDIT

Name

PROBLEM 4.2A or 4.2B (continued)

GENERAL LEDGER

ACCOUNT ______ ACCOUNT NO. ______

DATE		DESCRIPTION	POST. REF.	DEBIT	CREDIT	BALANCE DEBIT	BALANCE CREDIT

ACCOUNT ______ ACCOUNT NO. ______

DATE		DESCRIPTION	POST. REF.	DEBIT	CREDIT	BALANCE DEBIT	BALANCE CREDIT

ACCOUNT ______ ACCOUNT NO. ______

DATE		DESCRIPTION	POST. REF.	DEBIT	CREDIT	BALANCE DEBIT	BALANCE CREDIT

ACCOUNT ______ ACCOUNT NO. ______

DATE		DESCRIPTION	POST. REF.	DEBIT	CREDIT	BALANCE DEBIT	BALANCE CREDIT

Name

PROBLEM 4.2A or 4.2B (continued)

GENERAL LEDGER

ACCOUNT ______ ACCOUNT NO. ______

DATE		DESCRIPTION	POST. REF.	DEBIT	CREDIT	BALANCE DEBIT	BALANCE CREDIT

ACCOUNT ______ ACCOUNT NO. ______

DATE		DESCRIPTION	POST. REF.	DEBIT	CREDIT	BALANCE DEBIT	BALANCE CREDIT

ACCOUNT ______ ACCOUNT NO. ______

DATE		DESCRIPTION	POST. REF.	DEBIT	CREDIT	BALANCE DEBIT	BALANCE CREDIT

ACCOUNT ______ ACCOUNT NO. ______

DATE		DESCRIPTION	POST. REF.	DEBIT	CREDIT	BALANCE DEBIT	BALANCE CREDIT

ACCOUNT ______ ACCOUNT NO. ______

DATE		DESCRIPTION	POST. REF.	DEBIT	CREDIT	BALANCE DEBIT	BALANCE CREDIT

Name

PROBLEM 4.2A or 4.2B (continued)

GENERAL LEDGER

ACCOUNT ______ ACCOUNT NO. ______

DATE		DESCRIPTION	POST. REF.	DEBIT	CREDIT	BALANCE	
						DEBIT	CREDIT

ACCOUNT ______ ACCOUNT NO. ______

DATE		DESCRIPTION	POST. REF.	DEBIT	CREDIT	BALANCE	
						DEBIT	CREDIT

ACCOUNT ______ ACCOUNT NO. ______

DATE		DESCRIPTION	POST. REF.	DEBIT	CREDIT	BALANCE	
						DEBIT	CREDIT

ACCOUNT ______ ACCOUNT NO. ______

DATE		DESCRIPTION	POST. REF.	DEBIT	CREDIT	BALANCE	
						DEBIT	CREDIT

ACCOUNT ______ ACCOUNT NO. ______

DATE		DESCRIPTION	POST. REF.	DEBIT	CREDIT	BALANCE	
						DEBIT	CREDIT

Analyze:

Name

PROBLEM 4.3A or 4.3B

Analyze:

PROBLEM 4.4A or 4.4B

GENERAL JOURNAL PAGE

DATE		DESCRIPTION	POST. REF.	DEBIT	CREDIT

Name ____________________

PROBLEM 4.4A or 4.4B (continued)

GENERAL LEDGER

ACCOUNT ____________________ ACCOUNT NO. ________

DATE		DESCRIPTION	POST. REF.	DEBIT	CREDIT	BALANCE	
						DEBIT	CREDIT

ACCOUNT ____________________ ACCOUNT NO. ________

DATE		DESCRIPTION	POST. REF.	DEBIT	CREDIT	BALANCE	
						DEBIT	CREDIT

ACCOUNT ____________________ ACCOUNT NO. ________

DATE		DESCRIPTION	POST. REF.	DEBIT	CREDIT	BALANCE	
						DEBIT	CREDIT

ACCOUNT ____________________ ACCOUNT NO. ________

DATE		DESCRIPTION	POST. REF.	DEBIT	CREDIT	BALANCE	
						DEBIT	CREDIT

ACCOUNT ____________________ ACCOUNT NO. ________

DATE		DESCRIPTION	POST. REF.	DEBIT	CREDIT	BALANCE	
						DEBIT	CREDIT

Name

PROBLEM 4.4A or 4.4B (continued)

GENERAL LEDGER

ACCOUNT ______ ACCOUNT NO. ______

DATE		DESCRIPTION	POST. REF.	DEBIT	CREDIT	BALANCE DEBIT	BALANCE CREDIT

ACCOUNT ______ ACCOUNT NO. ______

DATE		DESCRIPTION	POST. REF.	DEBIT	CREDIT	BALANCE DEBIT	BALANCE CREDIT

ACCOUNT ______ ACCOUNT NO. ______

DATE		DESCRIPTION	POST. REF.	DEBIT	CREDIT	BALANCE DEBIT	BALANCE CREDIT

ACCOUNT ______ ACCOUNT NO. ______

DATE		DESCRIPTION	POST. REF.	DEBIT	CREDIT	BALANCE DEBIT	BALANCE CREDIT

Analyze: ______

EXTRA FORM

GENERAL LEDGER

ACCOUNT ______ ACCOUNT NO. ______

DATE		DESCRIPTION	POST. REF.	DEBIT	CREDIT	BALANCE DEBIT	BALANCE CREDIT

Name

CRITICAL THINKING PROBLEM 4.1

Name

CRITICAL THINKING PROBLEM 4.1 (continued)

Name

CRITICAL THINKING PROBLEM 4.2

GENERAL JOURNAL PAGE

DATE	DESCRIPTION	POST. REF.	DEBIT	CREDIT

Name ______________________

CRITICAL THINKING PROBLEM 4.2 (continued)

GENERAL JOURNAL

PAGE ______

DATE	DESCRIPTION	POST. REF.	DEBIT	CREDIT

Name

CRITICAL THINKING PROBLEM 4.2 (continued)

GENERAL JOURNAL

PAGE

	DATE		DESCRIPTION	POST. REF.	DEBIT	CREDIT	
1							1
2							2
3							3
4							4
5							5
6							6
7							7
8							8
9							9
10							10
11							11
12							12
13							13
14							14

GENERAL LEDGER

ACCOUNT ACCOUNT NO.

DATE		DESCRIPTION	POST. REF.	DEBIT	CREDIT	BALANCE	
						DEBIT	CREDIT

Name

CRITICAL THINKING PROBLEM 4.2 (continued)

GENERAL LEDGER

ACCOUNT ______________________ ACCOUNT NO. ________

DATE	DESCRIPTION	POST. REF.	DEBIT	CREDIT	BALANCE DEBIT	BALANCE CREDIT

ACCOUNT ______________________ ACCOUNT NO. ________

DATE	DESCRIPTION	POST. REF.	DEBIT	CREDIT	BALANCE DEBIT	BALANCE CREDIT

ACCOUNT ______________________ ACCOUNT NO. ________

DATE	DESCRIPTION	POST. REF.	DEBIT	CREDIT	BALANCE DEBIT	BALANCE CREDIT

ACCOUNT ______________________ ACCOUNT NO. ________

DATE	DESCRIPTION	POST. REF.	DEBIT	CREDIT	BALANCE DEBIT	BALANCE CREDIT

ACCOUNT ______________________ ACCOUNT NO. ________

DATE	DESCRIPTION	POST. REF.	DEBIT	CREDIT	BALANCE DEBIT	BALANCE CREDIT

Name ____________________

CRITICAL THINKING PROBLEM 4.2 (continued)

GENERAL LEDGER

ACCOUNT ____________________ ACCOUNT NO. ______

DATE		DESCRIPTION	POST. REF.	DEBIT	CREDIT	BALANCE DEBIT	BALANCE CREDIT

ACCOUNT ____________________ ACCOUNT NO. ______

DATE		DESCRIPTION	POST. REF.	DEBIT	CREDIT	BALANCE DEBIT	BALANCE CREDIT

ACCOUNT ____________________ ACCOUNT NO. ______

DATE		DESCRIPTION	POST. REF.	DEBIT	CREDIT	BALANCE DEBIT	BALANCE CREDIT

ACCOUNT ____________________ ACCOUNT NO. ______

DATE		DESCRIPTION	POST. REF.	DEBIT	CREDIT	BALANCE DEBIT	BALANCE CREDIT

ACCOUNT ____________________ ACCOUNT NO. ______

DATE		DESCRIPTION	POST. REF.	DEBIT	CREDIT	BALANCE DEBIT	BALANCE CREDIT

Name

CRITICAL THINKING PROBLEM 4.2 (continued)

GENERAL LEDGER

ACCOUNT ______ ACCOUNT NO. ______

DATE	DESCRIPTION	POST. REF.	DEBIT	CREDIT	BALANCE DEBIT	BALANCE CREDIT

ACCOUNT ______ ACCOUNT NO. ______

DATE	DESCRIPTION	POST. REF.	DEBIT	CREDIT	BALANCE DEBIT	BALANCE CREDIT

ACCOUNT ______ ACCOUNT NO. ______

DATE	DESCRIPTION	POST. REF.	DEBIT	CREDIT	BALANCE DEBIT	BALANCE CREDIT

EXTRA FORMS

GENERAL LEDGER

ACCOUNT ______ ACCOUNT NO. ______

DATE	DESCRIPTION	POST. REF.	DEBIT	CREDIT	BALANCE DEBIT	BALANCE CREDIT

ACCOUNT ______ ACCOUNT NO. ______

DATE	DESCRIPTION	POST. REF.	DEBIT	CREDIT	BALANCE DEBIT	BALANCE CREDIT

Name

CRITICAL THINKING PROBLEM 4.2 (continued)

ACCOUNT NAME	DEBIT	CREDIT

ACCOUNT NAME	DEBIT	CREDIT

Name

CRITICAL THINKING PROBLEM 4.2 (continued)

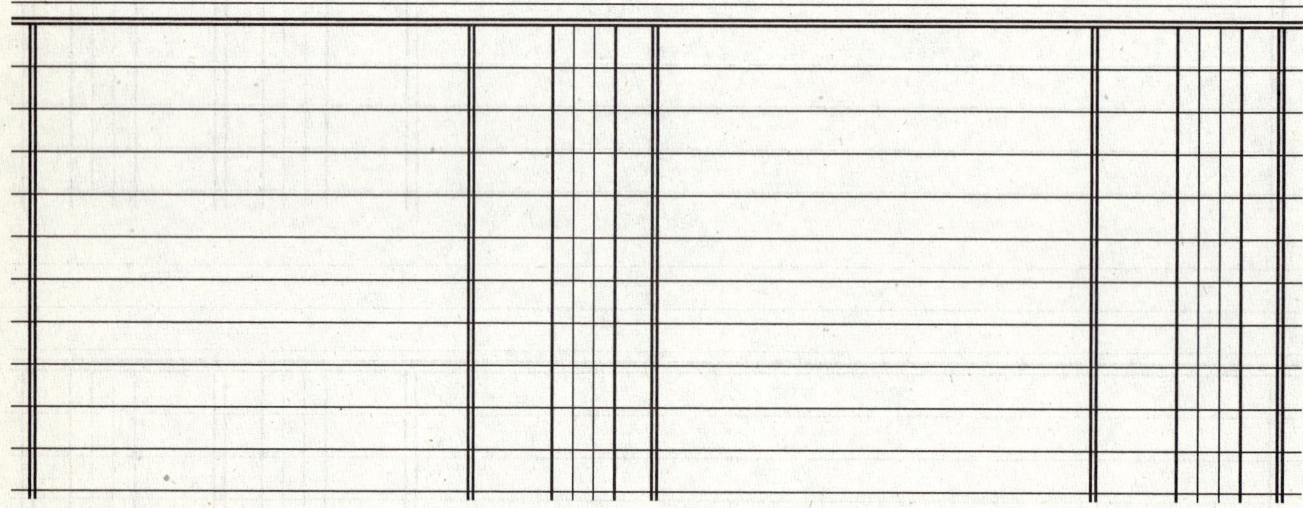

Analyze:

Chapter 4 Practice Test Answer Key

Part A Matching

1. i	**6.** g
2. h	**7.** a
3. d	**8.** f
4. e	**9.** b
5. c	**10.** j

Part B Completion

1. debit	**6.** ledger
2. year	**7.** posting references
3. chronological or date	**8.** brief or concise
4. assets or balance sheet accounts	**9.** credit
5. posted	**10.** debit

CHAPTER 5

Adjustments and the Worksheet

STUDY GUIDE

Understanding the Chapter

Objectives

1. Complete a trial balance on a worksheet. **2.** Prepare adjustments for unrecorded business transactions. **3.** Complete the worksheet. **4.** Prepare an income statement, statement of owner's equity, and balance sheet from the completed worksheet. **5.** Journalize and post the adjusting entries. **6.** Define the accounting terms new to this chapter.

Reading Assignment

Read Chapter 5 in the textbook. Complete the textbook Section Self Review as you finish reading each section of the chapter, and the Comprehensive Self Review at the end of the chapter. Refer to the Chapter 5 Glossary or to the Glossary at the end of the book to find definitions for terms that are not familiar to you.

Activities

- ❑ **Thinking Critically** — Answer the *Thinking Critically* questions for Boeing and Managerial Implications.
- ❑ **Discussion Questions** — Answer each assigned discussion question in Chapter 5.
- ❑ **Exercises** — Complete each assigned exercise in Chapter 5. Use the forms provided in this SGWP. The objectives covered by an exercise are given after the exercise number. If you need help with an exercise, review the portion of the chapter related to the objective(s) covered.
- ❑ **Problems A/B** — Complete each assigned problem in Chapter 5. Use the forms provided in this SGWP. The objectives covered by a problem are given after the problem number. If you need help with a problem, review the portion of the chapter related to the objective(s) covered.
- ❑ **Critical Thinking Problems** — Complete the critical thinking problems as assigned. Use the forms provided in this SGWP.
- ❑ **Business Connections** — Complete the Business Connections activities as assigned to gain a deeper understanding of Chapter 5 concepts.

Practice Tests

Complete the Practice Tests, which cover the main points in your reading assignment. Compare your answers with those in the Practice Test Answer Key for Chapter 5 at the end of this chapter. If you have answered any questions incorrectly, review the related section of the text.

Part A True-False *For each of the following statements, circle T in the answer column if the statement is true or F if the statement is false.*

T F 1. The balances of the expense accounts are normally transferred to the Income Statement Debit column of the worksheet.

T F 2. When the Balance Sheet columns of the worksheet are first added, the total of the Debit column should equal the total of the Credit column.

T F 3. After the net income (or net loss) is computed in the Income Statement section of the worksheet, this amount is transferred to the Balance Sheet section of the worksheet.

T F 4. On a worksheet, the difference between the Debit and Credit Column totals in the Income Statement section must equal the difference between the Debit and Credit column totals in the Balance Sheet section.

T F 5. The Income Statement columns and Balance Sheet columns provide the figures for preparing the financial statements.

T F 6. The ledger must be in balance before financial statements are prepared.

T F 7. Accountants use a worksheet as a means of organizing their figures quickly.

T F 8. The first two money columns of the worksheet contain a trial balance of the general ledger accounts.

T F 9. Asset account balances from the trial balance are normally transferred to the Income Statement Debit column of the worksheet.

T F 10. Liability account balances from the trial balance are normally transferred to the Balance Sheet credit column of the worksheet.

Part B Matching *For each numbered item, choose the matching term from the box and write the identifying letter in the answer column.*

a. Worksheet
b. Trial balance
c. Debit balance
d. Fundamental accounting equation
e. Credit balance
f. In balance

_______ **1.** A form used to organize the amounts needed to prepare the financial statements.

_______ **2.** The term used when referring to an account in which there is an excess of credits over debits.

_______ **3.** The term used when the total of the debit amounts in the general ledger and the total of the credit amounts are equal.

_______ **4.** The term used for an account with an excess of debits over credits.

_______ **5.** A way to test the accuracy of the figures recorded in the general ledger.

_______ **6.** Assets = Liabilities + Owner's Equity.

Demonstration Problem

The general ledger accounts listed on the worksheet for the Amos Graphics Design Company on January 31, 2013, show the results of the first month of operation.

Instructions

1. Record the following adjustments in the Adjustments section of the worksheet using the information below.
   - **a.** Supplies used during the month, $8,850.
   - **b.** The amount in the **Prepaid Rent** account represents a payment made on January 1 for the rent for 12 months.
   - **c.** The equipment, purchased in January, has an estimated useful life of 10 years with no salvage value. The firm uses the straight-line method of depreciation.
2. Complete the worksheet.
3. Journalize and post the adjusting entries. Use journal page number 2.

SOLUTION

Amos Graphics Design Company
Worksheet
Month Ended January 31, 2013

ACCOUNT NAME	TRIAL BALANCE		ADJUSTMENTS		ADJUSTED TRIAL BALANCE		INCOME STATEMENT		BALANCE SHEET	
	DEBIT	CREDIT	DEBIT	CREDIT	DEBIT	CREDIT	DEBIT	CREDIT	DEBIT	CREDIT
Cash	74,700.00				74,700.00				74,700.00	
Accounts Receivable	101,400.00				101,400.00				101,400.00	
Supplies	17,400.00			(a) 8,850.00	8,550.00				8,550.00	
Prepaid Rent	252,000.00			(b)21,000.00	231,000.00				231,000.00	
Equipment	252,000.00				252,000.00				252,000.00	
Accum. Depr.—Equipment				(c) 2,100.00		2,100.00				2,100.00
Accounts Payable		160,800.00				160,800.00				160,800.00
John Amos, Capital		295,200.00				295,200.00				295,200.00
John Amos, Drawing	18,000.00				18,000.00				18,000.00	
Fees Income		453,030.00				453,030.00		453,030.00		
Advertising Expense	22,800.00				22,800.00		22,800.00			
Insurance Expense	24,000.00				24,000.00		24,000.00			
Salaries Expense	135,000.00				135,000.00		135,000.00			
Supplies Expense			(a) 8,850.00		8,850.00		8,850.00			
Rent Expense			(b)21,000.00		21,000.00		21,000.00			
Telephone Expense	5,250.00				5,250.00		5,250.00			
Utilities Expense	6,480.00				6,480.00		6,480.00			
Depr. Expense—Equipment			(c) 2,100.00		2,100.00		2,100.00			
Totals	909,030.00	909,030.00	31,950.00	31,950.00	911,130.00	911,130.00	225,480.00	453,030.00	685,650.00	458,100.00
Net Income							227,550.00			227,550.00
							453,030.00	453,030.00	685,650.00	685,650.00

SOLUTION (continued)

GENERAL JOURNAL

PAGE 2

DATE		DESCRIPTION	POST. REF.	DEBIT	CREDIT
		Adjusting Entries			
2013					
Jan.	31	Supplies Expense	518	8,850.00	
		Supplies	121		8,850.00
	31	Rent Expense	519	21,000.00	
		Prepaid Rent	131		21,000.00
	31	Depreciation Expense—Equipment	524	2,100.00	
		Accumulated Depreciation—Equipment	142		2,100.00

GENERAL LEDGER (PARTIAL)

ACCOUNT **Supplies** ACCOUNT NO. **121**

DATE		DESCRIPTION	POST. REF.	DEBIT	CREDIT	BALANCE DEBIT	BALANCE CREDIT
2013							
Jan.	3		J1	17,400.00		17,400.00	
	31	Adjusting	J2		8,850.00	8,550.00	

ACCOUNT **Prepaid Rent** ACCOUNT NO. **131**

DATE		DESCRIPTION	POST. REF.	DEBIT	CREDIT	BALANCE DEBIT	BALANCE CREDIT
2013							
Jan.	2		J1	252,000.00		252,000.00	
	31	Adjusting	J2		21,000.00	231,000.00	

ACCOUNT **Accumulated Depreciation—Equipment** ACCOUNT NO. **142**

DATE		DESCRIPTION	POST. REF.	DEBIT	CREDIT	BALANCE DEBIT	BALANCE CREDIT
2013							
Jan.	31	Adjusting	J2		2,100.00		2,100.00

SOLUTION (continued)

GENERAL LEDGER (PARTIAL)

ACCOUNT **Supplies Expense** ACCOUNT NO. **518**

DATE		DESCRIPTION	POST. REF.	DEBIT	CREDIT	BALANCE DEBIT	BALANCE CREDIT
2013							
Jan.	**31**	**Adjusting**	**J2**	**8 8 5 0 00**		**8 8 5 0 00**	

ACCOUNT **Rent Expense** ACCOUNT NO. **519**

DATE		DESCRIPTION	POST. REF.	DEBIT	CREDIT	BALANCE DEBIT	BALANCE CREDIT
2013							
Jan.	**31**	**Adjusting**	**J2**	**21 0 0 0 00**		**21 0 0 0 00**	

ACCOUNT **Depreciation Expense—Equipment** ACCOUNT NO. **524**

DATE		DESCRIPTION	POST. REF.	DEBIT	CREDIT	BALANCE DEBIT	BALANCE CREDIT
2013							
Jan.	**31**	**Adjusting**	**J2**	**2 1 0 0 00**		**2 1 0 0 00**	

WORKING PAPERS

Name ______________________

EXERCISE 5.1

1. ______________________

2. ______________________

3. ______________________

EXERCISE 5.2

1. ______________________

2. ______________________

Name

EXERCISE 5.3

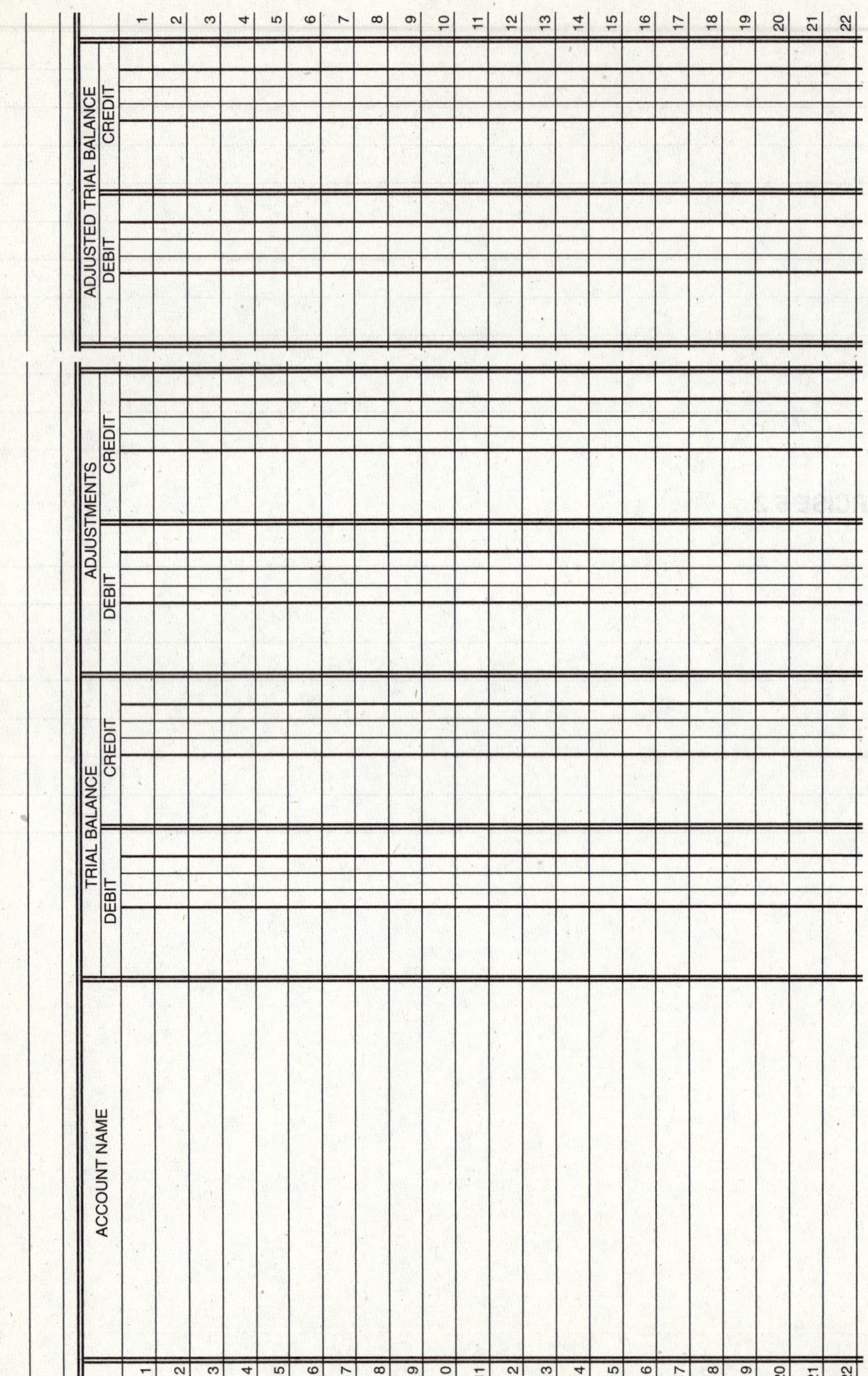

	ACCOUNT NAME	TRIAL BALANCE		ADJUSTMENTS		ADJUSTED TRIAL BALANCE		
		DEBIT	CREDIT	DEBIT	CREDIT	DEBIT	CREDIT	
1								1
2								2
3								3
4								4
5								5
6								6
7								7
8								8
9								9
10								10
11								11
12								12
13								13
14								14
15								15
16								16
17								17
18								18
19								19
20								20
21								21
22								22

Name

EXERCISE 5.4

Name

EXERCISE 5.5

GENERAL JOURNAL

PAGE

	DATE		DESCRIPTION	POST. REF.	DEBIT	CREDIT	
1							1
2							2
3							3
4							4
5							5
6							6
7							7
8							8
9							9
10							10
11							11

GENERAL LEDGER

ACCOUNT **Supplies** ACCOUNT NO. **121**

DATE		DESCRIPTION	POST. REF.	DEBIT	CREDIT	BALANCE	
						DEBIT	CREDIT

ACCOUNT **Prepaid Insurance** ACCOUNT NO. **131**

DATE		DESCRIPTION	POST. REF.	DEBIT	CREDIT	BALANCE	
						DEBIT	CREDIT

ACCOUNT **Accumulated Depreciation—Equipment** ACCOUNT NO. **142**

DATE		DESCRIPTION	POST. REF.	DEBIT	CREDIT	BALANCE	
						DEBIT	CREDIT

Name ______________________

EXERCISE 5.5 (continued)

GENERAL LEDGER

ACCOUNT **Depreciation Expense—Equipment** ACCOUNT NO. **517**

DATE	DESCRIPTION	POST. REF.	DEBIT	CREDIT	BALANCE DEBIT	BALANCE CREDIT

ACCOUNT **Insurance Expense** ACCOUNT NO. **521**

DATE	DESCRIPTION	POST. REF.	DEBIT	CREDIT	BALANCE DEBIT	BALANCE CREDIT

ACCOUNT **Supplies Expense** ACCOUNT NO. **523**

DATE	DESCRIPTION	POST. REF.	DEBIT	CREDIT	BALANCE DEBIT	BALANCE CREDIT

EXTRA FORMS

ACCOUNT ______________________ ACCOUNT NO. ________

DATE	DESCRIPTION	POST. REF.	DEBIT	CREDIT	BALANCE DEBIT	BALANCE CREDIT

ACCOUNT ______________________ ACCOUNT NO. ________

DATE	DESCRIPTION	POST. REF.	DEBIT	CREDIT	BALANCE DEBIT	BALANCE CREDIT

Name ______________________________

PROBLEM 5.1A or 5.1B

	ACCOUNT NAME	TRIAL BALANCE		ADJUSTMENTS	
		DEBIT	CREDIT	DEBIT	CREDIT
1					
2					
3					
4					
5					
6					
7					
8					
9					
10					
11					
12					
13					
14					
15					
16					
17					
18					
19					
20					
21					
22					
23					
24					
25					
26					
27					
28					
29					
30					
31					
32					

Name

PROBLEM 5.1A or 5.1B (continued)

ADJUSTED TRIAL BALANCE		INCOME STATEMENT		BALANCE SHEET		
DEBIT	CREDIT	DEBIT	CREDIT	DEBIT	CREDIT	
						1
						2
						3
						4
						5
						6
						7
						8
						9
						10
						11
						12
						13
						14
						15
						16
						17
						18
						19
						20
						21
						22
						23
						24
						25
						26
						27
						28
						29
						30
						31
						32

Analyze:

Name

PROBLEM 5.2A or 5.2B

	ACCOUNT NAME	TRIAL BALANCE		ADJUSTMENTS	
		DEBIT	CREDIT	DEBIT	CREDIT
1					
2					
3					
4					
5					
6					
7					
8					
9					
10					
11					
12					
13					
14					
15					
16					
17					
18					
19					
20					
21					
22					
23					
24					
25					
26					
27					
28					
29					
30					
31					
32					

Name

PROBLEM 5.2A or 5.2B (continued)

ADJUSTED TRIAL BALANCE		INCOME STATEMENT		BALANCE SHEET		
DEBIT	CREDIT	DEBIT	CREDIT	DEBIT	CREDIT	
						1
						2
						3
						4
						5
						6
						7
						8
						9
						10
						11
						12
						13
						14
						15
						16
						17
						18
						19
						20
						21
						22
						23
						24
						25
						26
						27
						28
						29
						30
						31
						32

Analyze:

Name

PROBLEM 5.3A or 5.3B

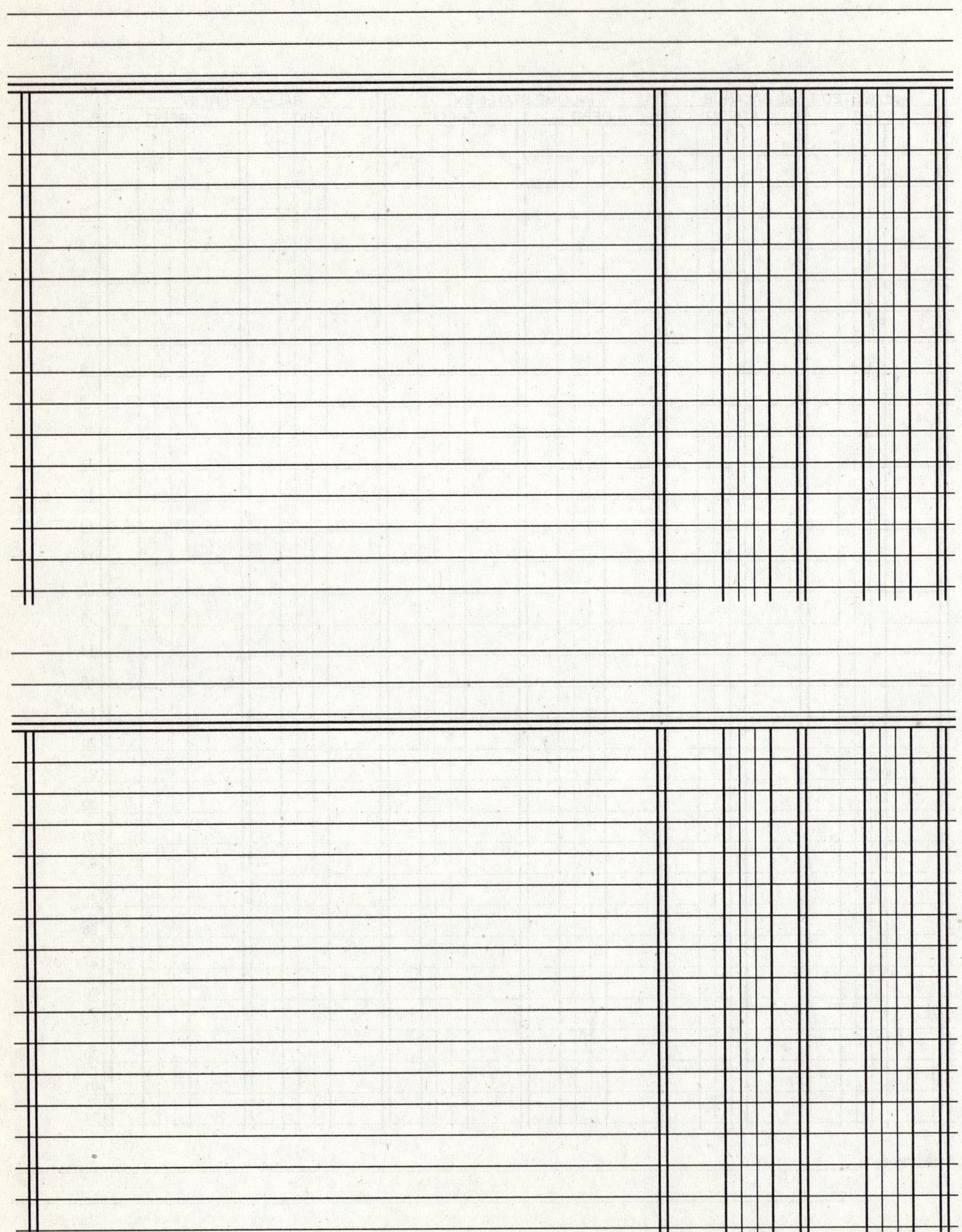

Name

PROBLEM 5.3A or 5.3B (continued)

Analyze:

Name ______________________

PROBLEM 5.4A or 5.4B

	ACCOUNT NAME	TRIAL BALANCE DEBIT	TRIAL BALANCE CREDIT	ADJUSTMENTS DEBIT	ADJUSTMENTS CREDIT
1					
2					
3					
4					
5					
6					
7					
8					
9					
10					
11					
12					
13					
14					
15					
16					
17					
18					
19					
20					
21					
22					
23					
24					
25					
26					
27					
28					
29					
30					
31					
32					

Name

PROBLEM 5.4A or 5.4B (continued)

ADJUSTED TRIAL BALANCE		INCOME STATEMENT		BALANCE SHEET		
DEBIT	CREDIT	DEBIT	CREDIT	DEBIT	CREDIT	
						1
						2
						3
						4
						5
						6
						7
						8
						9
						10
						11
						12
						13
						14
						15
						16
						17
						18
						19
						20
						21
						22
						23
						24
						25
						26
						27
						28
						29
						30
						31
						32

Name

PROBLEM 5.4A or 5.4B (continued)

Name

PROBLEM 5.4A or 5.4B (continued)

Name

PROBLEM 5.4A or 5.4B (continued)

GENERAL JOURNAL

PAGE

	DATE	DESCRIPTION	POST. REF.	DEBIT	CREDIT	
1						1
2						2
3						3
4						4
5						5
6						6
7						7
8						8
9						9
10						10
11						11
12						12
13						13
14						14

GENERAL LEDGER

ACCOUNT ACCOUNT NO.

DATE	DESCRIPTION	POST. REF.	DEBIT	CREDIT	BALANCE	
					DEBIT	CREDIT

ACCOUNT ACCOUNT NO.

DATE	DESCRIPTION	POST. REF.	DEBIT	CREDIT	BALANCE	
					DEBIT	CREDIT

ACCOUNT ACCOUNT NO.

DATE	DESCRIPTION	POST. REF.	DEBIT	CREDIT	BALANCE	
					DEBIT	CREDIT

Name ____________________

PROBLEM 5.4A or 5.4B (continued)

GENERAL LEDGER

ACCOUNT ____________________ ACCOUNT NO. ______

DATE		DESCRIPTION	POST. REF.	DEBIT	CREDIT	BALANCE	
						DEBIT	CREDIT

ACCOUNT ____________________ ACCOUNT NO. ______

DATE		DESCRIPTION	POST. REF.	DEBIT	CREDIT	BALANCE	
						DEBIT	CREDIT

ACCOUNT ____________________ ACCOUNT NO. ______

DATE		DESCRIPTION	POST. REF.	DEBIT	CREDIT	BALANCE	
						DEBIT	CREDIT

ACCOUNT ____________________ ACCOUNT NO. ______

DATE		DESCRIPTION	POST. REF.	DEBIT	CREDIT	BALANCE	
						DEBIT	CREDIT

ACCOUNT ____________________ ACCOUNT NO. ______

DATE		DESCRIPTION	POST. REF.	DEBIT	CREDIT	BALANCE	
						DEBIT	CREDIT

Analyze: ____________________

Name ______________________

CRITICAL THINKING PROBLEM 5.1

	ACCOUNT NAME	TRIAL BALANCE DEBIT	TRIAL BALANCE CREDIT	ADJUSTMENTS DEBIT	ADJUSTMENTS CREDIT
1					
2					
3					
4					
5					
6					
7					
8					
9					
10					
11					
12					
13					
14					
15					
16					
17					
18					
19					
20					
21					
22					
23					
24					
25					
26					
27					
28					
29					
30					
31					
32					

Name

CRITICAL THINKING PROBLEM 5.1 (continued)

ADJUSTED TRIAL BALANCE		INCOME STATEMENT		BALANCE SHEET	
DEBIT	CREDIT	DEBIT	CREDIT	DEBIT	CREDIT

Name

CRITICAL THINKING PROBLEM 5.1 (continued)

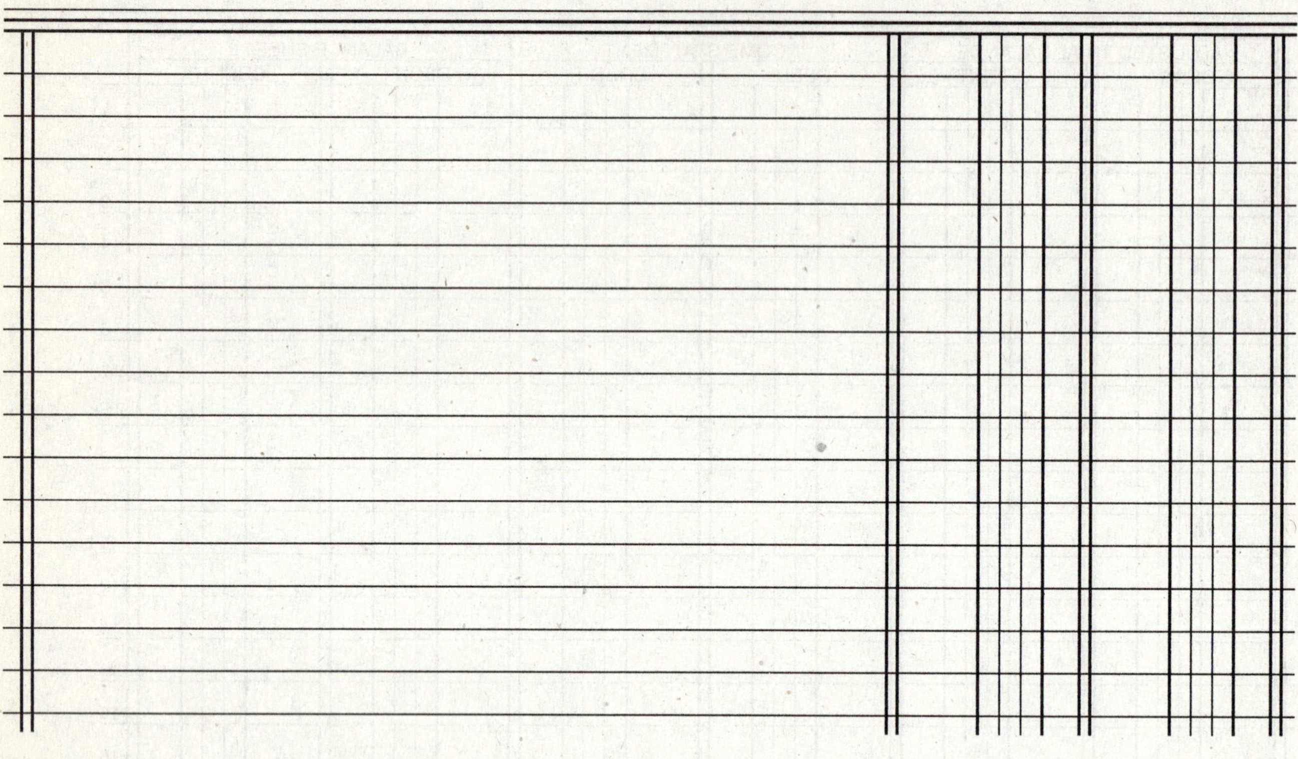

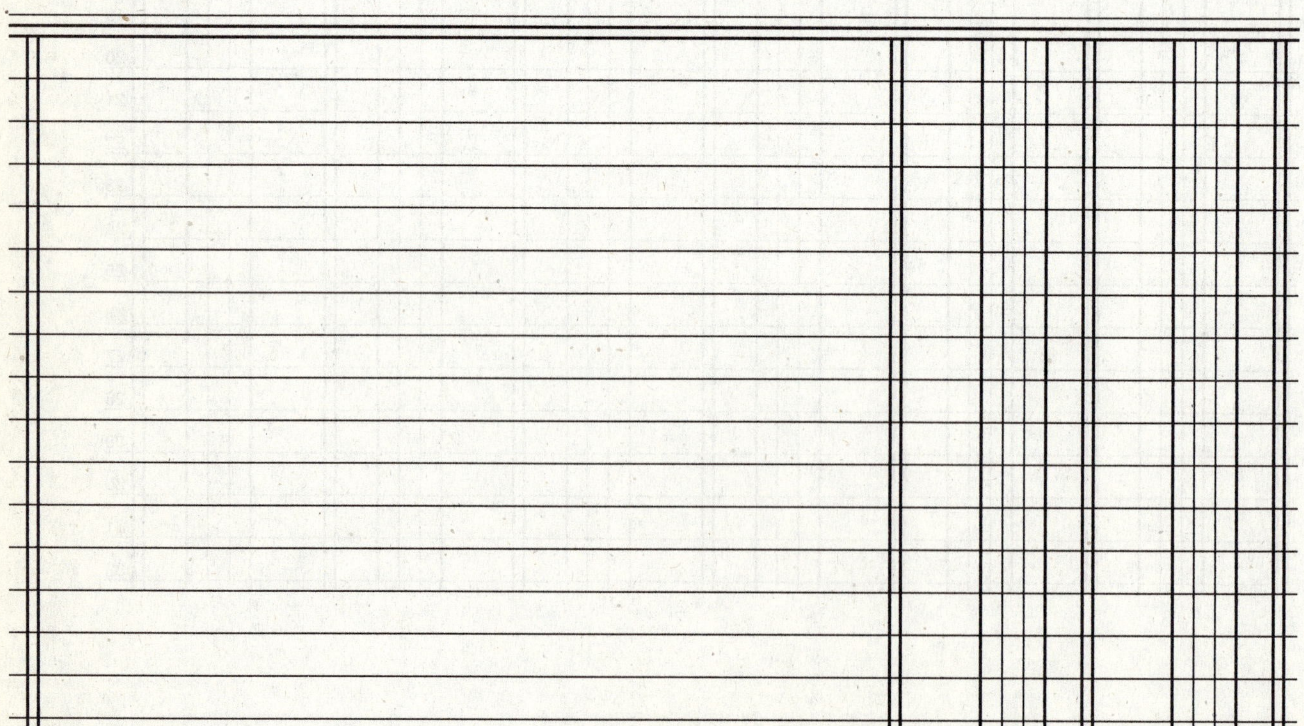

Name

CRITICAL THINKING PROBLEM 5.1 (continued)

Name ____________________

CRITICAL THINKING PROBLEM 5.1 (continued)

GENERAL JOURNAL

PAGE ____

	DATE		DESCRIPTION	POST. REF.	DEBIT	CREDIT	
1							1
2							2
3							3
4							4
5							5
6							6
7							7
8							8
9							9
10							10
11							11

GENERAL LEDGER

ACCOUNT ____________________ ACCOUNT NO. ________

DATE		DESCRIPTION	POST. REF.	DEBIT	CREDIT	BALANCE	
						DEBIT	CREDIT

ACCOUNT ____________________ ACCOUNT NO. ________

DATE		DESCRIPTION	POST. REF.	DEBIT	CREDIT	BALANCE	
						DEBIT	CREDIT

ACCOUNT ____________________ ACCOUNT NO. ________

DATE		DESCRIPTION	POST. REF.	DEBIT	CREDIT	BALANCE	
						DEBIT	CREDIT

Name ______________________

CRITICAL THINKING PROBLEM 5.1 (continued)

GENERAL LEDGER

ACCOUNT ______________________ ACCOUNT NO. ________

DATE		DESCRIPTION	POST. REF.	DEBIT	CREDIT	BALANCE DEBIT	BALANCE CREDIT

ACCOUNT ______________________ ACCOUNT NO. ________

DATE		DESCRIPTION	POST. REF.	DEBIT	CREDIT	BALANCE DEBIT	BALANCE CREDIT

ACCOUNT ______________________ ACCOUNT NO. ________

DATE		DESCRIPTION	POST. REF.	DEBIT	CREDIT	BALANCE DEBIT	BALANCE CREDIT

Analyze: ______________________

____

EXTRA FORMS

ACCOUNT ______________________ ACCOUNT NO. ________

DATE		DESCRIPTION	POST. REF.	DEBIT	CREDIT	BALANCE DEBIT	BALANCE CREDIT

ACCOUNT ______________________ ACCOUNT NO. ________

DATE		DESCRIPTION	POST. REF.	DEBIT	CREDIT	BALANCE DEBIT	BALANCE CREDIT

Name

CRITICAL THINKING PROBLEM 5.2

TO:

FROM:

DATE:

SUBJECT:

Chapter 5 Practice Test Answer Key

Part A True-False

1. T	**6. T**
2. F	**7. T**
3. T	**8. T**
4. T	**9. F**
5. T	**10. T**

Part B Matching

1. a	**4. c**
2. e	**5. b**
3. f	**6. d**

CHAPTER 6

Closing Entries and the Postclosing Trial Balance

STUDY GUIDE

STUDY GUIDE

Understanding the Chapter

Objectives

1. Journalize and post closing entries. **2.** Prepare a postclosing trial balance. **3.** Interpret financial statements. **4.** Review the steps in the accounting cycle. **5.** Define the accounting terms new to this chapter.

Reading Assignment

Read Chapter 6 in the textbook. Complete the textbook Section Self Review as you finish reading each section of the chapter, and the Comprehensive Self Review at the end of the chapter. Refer to the Chapter 6 Glossary or to the Glossary at the end of the book to find definitions for terms that are not familiar to you.

Activities

- ❑ **Thinking Critically** — Answer the *Thinking Critically* questions for Carnival Corporation and Managerial Implications.
- ❑ **Discussion Questions** — Answer each assigned discussion question in Chapter 6.
- ❑ **Exercises** — Complete each assigned exercise in Chapter 6. Use the forms provided in this SGWP. The objectives covered by an exercise are given after the exercise number. If you need help with an exercise, review the portion of the chapter related to the objective(s) covered.
- ❑ **Problems A/B** — Complete each assigned problem in Chapter 6. Use the forms provided in this SGWP. The objectives covered by a problem are given after the problem number. If you need help with a problem, review the portion of the chapter related to the objective(s) covered.
- ❑ **Critical Thinking Problems** — Complete the critical thinking problems as assigned. Use the forms provided in this SGWP.
- ❑ **Business Connections** — Complete the Business Connections activities as assigned to gain a deeper understanding of Chapter 6 concepts.

Practice Tests

Complete the Practice Tests, which cover the main points in your reading assignment. Compare your answers with those in the Practice Test Answer Key for Chapter 6 at the end of this chapter. If you have answered any questions incorrectly, review the related section of the text.

Part A True-False *For each of the following statements, circle T in the answer column if the statement is true or F if the statement is false.*

T F 1. The general ledger is a continuing record.

T F 2. The postclosing trial balance will show figures for asset, liability, owner's equity, revenue, and expense accounts.

T F 3. The total of all expenses appears on the credit side of the **Income Summary** account.

T F 4. To close a revenue account, the accountant debits that account and credits the **Income Summary** account.

T F 5. All asset accounts are closed into the **Income Summary** account.

T F 6. The balance of the **Income Summary** account—net income or net loss—is transferred to the owner's capital account.

T F 7. The Income Summary is a financial statement prepared at the end of each accounting period.

T F 8. Adjusting entries create a permanent record of any changes in account balances that are shown on the worksheet.

T F 9. If an adjustment is not made for supplies used, the net income for the period will be understated.

T F 10. Closing entries reduce the balance of revenue and asset accounts to zero so that they are ready to receive data for the next period.

Part B Matching *For each numbered item, choose the matching term from the box and write the identifying letter in the answer column.*

______ 1. The procedure of journalizing and posting the results of operations at the end of an accounting period.

______ 2. Journal entries used to transfer the balances of the revenue and expense accounts to the summary accounts as part of the end-of-period procedures.

______ 3. Term used when referring to an account after its balance has been transferred out.

______ 4. Special account in the general ledger used for combining data about revenue and expenses.

______ 5. The last step in the end-of-period procedure, which shows the accountant that it is safe to proceed with entries for the new period.

a. Closing the accounting records
b. Closing entries
c. Closed account
d. Postclosing trial balance
e. Income Summary

Demonstration Problem

The Income Statement and Balance Sheet sections of the worksheet for James Wilson for the period ended December 31, 2013 are shown below.

Instructions

1. Journalize the closing entries on page 24 of a general journal.
2. Determine the new balance for Capital once the closing entries have been posted.

James Wilson

Worksheet

Month Ended December 31, 2013

	ACCOUNT NAME	INCOME STATEMENT		BALANCE SHEET	
		DEBIT	CREDIT	DEBIT	CREDIT
1	**Cash**			96 000 00	
2	**Accounts Receivable**			6 000 00	
3	**Supplies**			12 000 00	
4	**Prepaid Rent**			9 000 00	
5	**Equipment**			60 000 00	
6	**Accumulated Depreciation—Equipment**				1 440 00
7	**Accounts Payable**				15 000 00
8	**James Wilson, Capital**				109 500 00
9	**James Wilson, Drawing**			6 000 00	
10	**Fees Income**		90 000 00		
11	**Salaries Expense**	14 400 00			
12	**Utilities Expense**	2 100 00			
13	**Supplies Expense**	4 800 00			
14	**Advertising Expense**	4 200 00			
15	**Depreciation Expense—Equipment**	1 440 00			
16	**Totals**	26 940 00	90 000 00	189 000 00	125 940 00
17	**Net Income**	63 060 00			63 060 00
18		90 000 00	90 000 00	189 000 00	189 000 00
19					

SOLUTION

GENERAL JOURNAL PAGE 24

DATE		DESCRIPTION	POST. REF.	DEBIT	CREDIT
		Closing Entries			
2013					
Dec.	31	Fees Income	401	90,000.00	
		Income Summary	399		90,000.00
	31	Income Summary	399	26,940.00	
		Salaries Expense	511		14,400.00
		Utilities Expense	514		2,100.00
		Supplies Expense	517		4,800.00
		Advertising Expense	522		4,200.00
		Depreciation Expense—Equipment	523		1,440.00
	31	Income Summary	399	63,060.00	
		James Wilson, Capital	301		63,060.00
	31	James Wilson, Capital	301	6,000.00	
		James Wilson, Drawing	302		6,000.00

New Capital Balance:		
James Wilson, Capital, December 1, 2013		$109,500.00
Add: Net Income	63,060.00	
Less Withdrawals for December	6,000.00	
Increase in Capital		57,060.00
James Wilson, Capital, December 31, 2013		$166,560.00

WORKING PAPERS

Name ____________________

EXERCISE 6.1

GENERAL JOURNAL

PAGE ____

	DATE		DESCRIPTION	POST. REF.	DEBIT	CREDIT	
1							1
2							2
3							3
4							4
5							5
6							6
7							7
8							8
9							9
10							10
11							11
12							12
13							13
14							14
15							15
16							16
17							17
18							18
19							19
20							20
21							21

EXERCISE 6.2

1. ____________________
2. ____________________
3. ____________________
4. ____________________
5. ____________________
6. ____________________
7. ____________________
8. ____________________
9. ____________________

Name ________________________________

EXERCISE 6.3

1. ______________________
2. ______________________
3. ______________________
4. ______________________
5. ______________________
6. ______________________
7. ______________________

EXERCISE 6.4

1. ______________
2. ______________
3. ______________
4. ______________
5. ______________
6. ______________
7. ______________
8. ______________
9. ______________
10. ______________
11. ______________
12. ______________
13. ______________
14. ______________
15. ______________

EXERCISE 6.5

1. Total revenue for the period is __________.

2. Total expenses for the period are __________.

3. Net income for the period is __________.

4. Owner's withdrawals for the period are __________.

Name

EXERCISE 6.6

GENERAL JOURNAL

PAGE

DATE		DESCRIPTION	POST. REF.	DEBIT	CREDIT

Name

EXERCISE 6.6 (continued)

GENERAL LEDGER

ACCOUNT Gloria Bahamon, Capital ACCOUNT NO. 301

DATE		DESCRIPTION	POST. REF.	DEBIT	CREDIT	BALANCE DEBIT	BALANCE CREDIT
2013							
Mar.	31	Balance	✔				120 0 0 0 00

ACCOUNT Gloria Bahamon, Drawing ACCOUNT NO. 302

DATE		DESCRIPTION	POST. REF.	DEBIT	CREDIT	BALANCE DEBIT	BALANCE CREDIT
2013							
Mar.	31	Balance	✔			12 0 0 0 00	

ACCOUNT Income Summary ACCOUNT NO. 399

DATE		DESCRIPTION	POST. REF.	DEBIT	CREDIT	BALANCE DEBIT	BALANCE CREDIT

ACCOUNT Fees Income ACCOUNT NO. 401

DATE		DESCRIPTION	POST. REF.	DEBIT	CREDIT	BALANCE DEBIT	BALANCE CREDIT
2013							
Mar.	31	Balance	✔				325 0 0 0 00

ACCOUNT Depreciation Expense—Equipment ACCOUNT NO. 510

DATE		DESCRIPTION	POST. REF.	DEBIT	CREDIT	BALANCE DEBIT	BALANCE CREDIT
2013							
Mar.	31	Balance	✔			20 1 6 0 00	

Name

EXERCISE 6.6 (continued)

GENERAL LEDGER

ACCOUNT Insurance Expense ACCOUNT NO. 511

DATE		DESCRIPTION	POST. REF.	DEBIT	CREDIT	BALANCE DEBIT	BALANCE CREDIT
2013							
Mar.	31	Balance	✔			10 4 0 0 00	

ACCOUNT Rent Expense ACCOUNT NO. 514

DATE		DESCRIPTION	POST. REF.	DEBIT	CREDIT	BALANCE DEBIT	BALANCE CREDIT
2013							
Mar.	31	Balance	✔			32 0 0 0 00	

ACCOUNT Salaries Expense ACCOUNT NO. 517

DATE		DESCRIPTION	POST. REF.	DEBIT	CREDIT	BALANCE DEBIT	BALANCE CREDIT
2013							
Mar.	31	Balance	✔			156 0 0 0 00	

ACCOUNT Supplies Expense ACCOUNT NO. 518

DATE		DESCRIPTION	POST. REF.	DEBIT	CREDIT	BALANCE DEBIT	BALANCE CREDIT
2013							
Mar.	31	Balance	✔			4 6 0 0 00	

ACCOUNT Telephone Expense ACCOUNT NO. 519

DATE		DESCRIPTION	POST. REF.	DEBIT	CREDIT	BALANCE DEBIT	BALANCE CREDIT
2013							
Mar.	31	Balance	✔			5 8 0 0 00	

Name

EXERCISE 6.6 (continued)

GENERAL LEDGER

ACCOUNT Utilities Expense ACCOUNT NO. 523

DATE		DESCRIPTION	POST. REF.	DEBIT	CREDIT	BALANCE DEBIT	BALANCE CREDIT
2013							
Mar.	31	Balance	✓			8,400.00	

EXTRA FORMS

ACCOUNT ACCOUNT NO.

DATE	DESCRIPTION	POST. REF.	DEBIT	CREDIT	BALANCE DEBIT	BALANCE CREDIT

ACCOUNT ACCOUNT NO.

DATE	DESCRIPTION	POST. REF.	DEBIT	CREDIT	BALANCE DEBIT	BALANCE CREDIT

ACCOUNT ACCOUNT NO.

DATE	DESCRIPTION	POST. REF.	DEBIT	CREDIT	BALANCE DEBIT	BALANCE CREDIT

Name

EXERCISE 6.7

GENERAL JOURNAL PAGE

	DATE		DESCRIPTION	POST. REF.	DEBIT	CREDIT	
1							1
2							2
3							3
4							4
5							5
6							6
7							7
8							8

EXERCISE 6.8

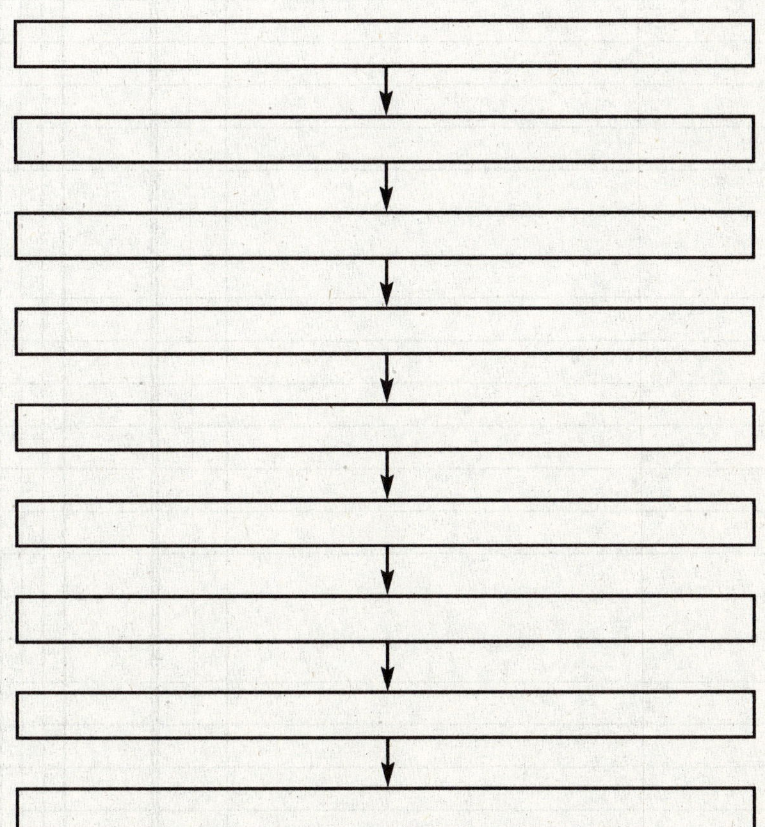

Name ____________________

PROBLEM 6.1A or 6.1B

GENERAL JOURNAL

PAGE ________

DATE		DESCRIPTION	POST. REF.	DEBIT	CREDIT

GENERAL JOURNAL

PAGE ________

DATE		DESCRIPTION	POST. REF.	DEBIT	CREDIT

Analyze: ____________________

Name ______________________

PROBLEM 6.2A or 6.2B

GENERAL JOURNAL

PAGE ______

	DATE		DESCRIPTION	POST. REF.	DEBIT	CREDIT	
1							1
2							2
3							3
4							4
5							5
6							6
7							7
8							8
9							9
10							10
11							11

GENERAL JOURNAL

PAGE ______

	DATE		DESCRIPTION	POST. REF.	DEBIT	CREDIT	
1							1
2							2
3							3
4							4
5							5
6							6
7							7
8							8
9							9
10							10
11							11
12							12
13							13
14							14
15							15
16							16
17							17
18							18

Name

PROBLEM 6.2A or 6.2B (continued)

GENERAL LEDGER

ACCOUNT **Supplies** ACCOUNT NO. **121**

DATE	DESCRIPTION	POST. REF.	DEBIT	CREDIT	BALANCE DEBIT	BALANCE CREDIT

ACCOUNT **Prepaid Advertising** ACCOUNT NO. **131**

DATE	DESCRIPTION	POST. REF.	DEBIT	CREDIT	BALANCE DEBIT	BALANCE CREDIT

ACCOUNT **Accumulated Depreciation—Equipment** ACCOUNT NO. **142**

DATE	DESCRIPTION	POST. REF.	DEBIT	CREDIT	BALANCE DEBIT	BALANCE CREDIT

ACCOUNT **Capital** ACCOUNT NO. **301**

DATE	DESCRIPTION	POST. REF.	DEBIT	CREDIT	BALANCE DEBIT	BALANCE CREDIT

ACCOUNT **Drawing** ACCOUNT NO. **302**

DATE	DESCRIPTION	POST. REF.	DEBIT	CREDIT	BALANCE DEBIT	BALANCE CREDIT

Name

PROBLEM 6.2A or 6.2B (continued)

GENERAL LEDGER

ACCOUNT **Income Summary** ACCOUNT NO. **399**

DATE		DESCRIPTION	POST. REF.	DEBIT	CREDIT	BALANCE DEBIT	BALANCE CREDIT

ACCOUNT **Fees Income** ACCOUNT NO. **401**

DATE		DESCRIPTION	POST. REF.	DEBIT	CREDIT	BALANCE DEBIT	BALANCE CREDIT

GENERAL LEDGER

ACCOUNT **Salaries Expense** ACCOUNT NO. **511**

DATE		DESCRIPTION	POST. REF.	DEBIT	CREDIT	BALANCE DEBIT	BALANCE CREDIT

ACCOUNT **Utilities Expense** ACCOUNT NO. **514**

DATE		DESCRIPTION	POST. REF.	DEBIT	CREDIT	BALANCE DEBIT	BALANCE CREDIT

ACCOUNT **Supplies Expense** ACCOUNT NO. **517**

DATE		DESCRIPTION	POST. REF.	DEBIT	CREDIT	BALANCE DEBIT	BALANCE CREDIT

Name

PROBLEM 6.2A or 6.2B (continued)

ACCOUNT **Depreciation Expense—Equipment** ACCOUNT NO. **523**

DATE		DESCRIPTION	POST. REF.	DEBIT	CREDIT	BALANCE DEBIT	BALANCE CREDIT

ACCOUNT **Advertising Expense** ACCOUNT NO. **526**

DATE		DESCRIPTION	POST. REF.	DEBIT	CREDIT	BALANCE DEBIT	BALANCE CREDIT

ACCOUNT NAME	DEBIT	CREDIT

Analyze:

Name ____________________

PROBLEM 6.3A or 6.3B

GENERAL JOURNAL

PAGE ______

DATE	DESCRIPTION	POST. REF.	DEBIT	CREDIT

Name

PROBLEM 6.3A or 6.3B (continued)

GENERAL LEDGER

ACCOUNT **Capital** ACCOUNT NO. **301**

DATE		DESCRIPTION	POST. REF.	DEBIT	CREDIT	BALANCE DEBIT	BALANCE CREDIT

ACCOUNT **Drawing** ACCOUNT NO. **302**

DATE		DESCRIPTION	POST. REF.	DEBIT	CREDIT	BALANCE DEBIT	BALANCE CREDIT

ACCOUNT **Income Summary** ACCOUNT NO. **399**

DATE		DESCRIPTION	POST. REF.	DEBIT	CREDIT	BALANCE DEBIT	BALANCE CREDIT

ACCOUNT **Fees Income** ACCOUNT NO. **401**

DATE		DESCRIPTION	POST. REF.	DEBIT	CREDIT	BALANCE DEBIT	BALANCE CREDIT

Name

PROBLEM 6.3A or 6.3B (continued)

GENERAL LEDGER

ACCOUNT **Advertising Expense** ACCOUNT NO. **511**

DATE	DESCRIPTION	POST. REF.	DEBIT	CREDIT	BALANCE DEBIT	BALANCE CREDIT

ACCOUNT **Depreciation Expense—Equipment** ACCOUNT NO. **514**

DATE	DESCRIPTION	POST. REF.	DEBIT	CREDIT	BALANCE DEBIT	BALANCE CREDIT

ACCOUNT **Rent Expense** ACCOUNT NO. **517**

DATE	DESCRIPTION	POST. REF.	DEBIT	CREDIT	BALANCE DEBIT	BALANCE CREDIT

ACCOUNT **Salaries Expense** ACCOUNT NO. **519**

DATE	DESCRIPTION	POST. REF.	DEBIT	CREDIT	BALANCE DEBIT	BALANCE CREDIT

ACCOUNT **Utilities Expense** ACCOUNT NO. **523**

DATE	DESCRIPTION	POST. REF.	DEBIT	CREDIT	BALANCE DEBIT	BALANCE CREDIT

Analyze:

Name ______________________

PROBLEM 6.3A or 6.3B (continued)

GENERAL LEDGER

ACCOUNT ______________________ ACCOUNT NO. ________

DATE	DESCRIPTION	POST. REF.	DEBIT	CREDIT	BALANCE	
					DEBIT	CREDIT

ACCOUNT ______________________ ACCOUNT NO. ________

DATE	DESCRIPTION	POST. REF.	DEBIT	CREDIT	BALANCE	
					DEBIT	CREDIT

ACCOUNT ______________________ ACCOUNT NO. ________

DATE	DESCRIPTION	POST. REF.	DEBIT	CREDIT	BALANCE	
					DEBIT	CREDIT

ACCOUNT ______________________ ACCOUNT NO. ________

DATE	DESCRIPTION	POST. REF.	DEBIT	CREDIT	BALANCE	
					DEBIT	CREDIT

ACCOUNT ______________________ ACCOUNT NO. ________

DATE	DESCRIPTION	POST. REF.	DEBIT	CREDIT	BALANCE	
					DEBIT	CREDIT

Name

PROBLEM 6.3A or 6.3B (continued)

GENERAL LEDGER

ACCOUNT ACCOUNT NO.

DATE		DESCRIPTION	POST. REF.	DEBIT	CREDIT	BALANCE DEBIT	BALANCE CREDIT

ACCOUNT ACCOUNT NO.

DATE		DESCRIPTION	POST. REF.	DEBIT	CREDIT	BALANCE DEBIT	BALANCE CREDIT

ACCOUNT ACCOUNT NO.

DATE		DESCRIPTION	POST. REF.	DEBIT	CREDIT	BALANCE DEBIT	BALANCE CREDIT

ACCOUNT ACCOUNT NO.

DATE		DESCRIPTION	POST. REF.	DEBIT	CREDIT	BALANCE DEBIT	BALANCE CREDIT

ACCOUNT ACCOUNT NO.

DATE		DESCRIPTION	POST. REF.	DEBIT	CREDIT	BALANCE DEBIT	BALANCE CREDIT

Name ______________________________

PROBLEM 6.4A or 6.4B

	ACCOUNT NAME	TRIAL BALANCE		ADJUSTMENTS	
		DEBIT	CREDIT	DEBIT	CREDIT
1					
2					
3					
4					
5					
6					
7					
8					
9					
10					
11					
12					
13					
14					
15					
16					
17					
18					
19					
20					
21					
22					
23					
24					
25					
26					
27					
28					
29					
30					
31					
32					

Name

PROBLEM 6.4A or 6.4B (continued)

ADJUSTED TRIAL BALANCE		INCOME STATEMENT		BALANCE SHEET	
DEBIT	CREDIT	DEBIT	CREDIT	DEBIT	CREDIT

Name

PROBLEM 6.4A or 6.4B (continued)

GENERAL JOURNAL PAGE

	DATE		DESCRIPTION	POST. REF.	DEBIT	CREDIT	
1							1
2							2
3							3
4							4
5							5
6							6
7							7
8							8
9							9
10							10
11							11
12							12
13							13

GENERAL JOURNAL PAGE

	DATE		DESCRIPTION	POST. REF.	DEBIT	CREDIT	
1							1
2							2
3							3
4							4
5							5
6							6
7							7
8							8
9							9
10							10
11							11
12							12
13							13
14							14
15							15
16							16
17							17
18							18

Name

PROBLEM 6.4A or 6.4B (continued)

GENERAL LEDGER

ACCOUNT **Supplies** ACCOUNT NO. **121**

DATE	DESCRIPTION	POST. REF.	DEBIT	CREDIT	BALANCE DEBIT	BALANCE CREDIT

ACCOUNT **Prepaid Advertising** ACCOUNT NO. **131**

DATE	DESCRIPTION	POST. REF.	DEBIT	CREDIT	BALANCE DEBIT	BALANCE CREDIT

ACCOUNT **Accumulated Depreciation—** ACCOUNT NO. **142**

DATE	DESCRIPTION	POST. REF.	DEBIT	CREDIT	BALANCE DEBIT	BALANCE CREDIT

ACCOUNT **Capital** ACCOUNT NO. **301**

DATE	DESCRIPTION	POST. REF.	DEBIT	CREDIT	BALANCE DEBIT	BALANCE CREDIT

ACCOUNT **Drawing** ACCOUNT NO. **302**

DATE	DESCRIPTION	POST. REF.	DEBIT	CREDIT	BALANCE DEBIT	BALANCE CREDIT

Name

PROBLEM 6.4A or 6.4B (continued)

GENERAL LEDGER

ACCOUNT Income Summary — ACCOUNT NO. 399

DATE		DESCRIPTION	POST. REF.	DEBIT	CREDIT	BALANCE	
						DEBIT	CREDIT

ACCOUNT Fees Income — ACCOUNT NO. 401

DATE		DESCRIPTION	POST. REF.	DEBIT	CREDIT	BALANCE	
						DEBIT	CREDIT

GENERAL LEDGER

ACCOUNT Salaries Expense — ACCOUNT NO. 511

DATE		DESCRIPTION	POST. REF.	DEBIT	CREDIT	BALANCE	
						DEBIT	CREDIT

ACCOUNT Utilities Expense — ACCOUNT NO. 514

DATE		DESCRIPTION	POST. REF.	DEBIT	CREDIT	BALANCE	
						DEBIT	CREDIT

ACCOUNT Supplies Expense — ACCOUNT NO. 517

DATE		DESCRIPTION	POST. REF.	DEBIT	CREDIT	BALANCE	
						DEBIT	CREDIT

Name ______________________

PROBLEM 6.4A or 6.4B (continued)

ACCOUNT **Depreciation Expense—** ACCOUNT NO. **523**

DATE		DESCRIPTION	POST. REF.	DEBIT	CREDIT	BALANCE DEBIT	BALANCE CREDIT

ACCOUNT **Advertising Expense** ACCOUNT NO. **526**

DATE		DESCRIPTION	POST. REF.	DEBIT	CREDIT	BALANCE DEBIT	BALANCE CREDIT

ACCOUNT NAME	DEBIT	CREDIT

Analyze: ______________________

Name

CRITICAL THINKING PROBLEM 6.1

Contemporary Fashions
Worksheet
Month Ended December 31, 2013

	ACCOUNT NAME	TRIAL BALANCE		ADJUSTMENTS	
		DEBIT	CREDIT	DEBIT	CREDIT
1	Cash	163,200.00			
2	Accounts Receivable	36,000.00			
3	Supplies	28,800.00			(a) 14,400.00
4	Prepaid Insurance	43,200.00			(b) 9,600.00
5	Machinery	336,000.00			
6	Accumulated Depreciation—Machinery				(c) 4,800.00
7	Accounts Payable		54,000.00		
8	Jada McBride, Capital		298,320.00		
9	Jada McBride, Drawing	24,000.00			
10	Fees Income		330,000.00		
11	Supplies Expense			(a) 14,400.00	
12	Insurance Expense			(b) 9,600.00	
13	Salaries Expense	44,400.00			
14	Depreciation Expense—Machinery			(c) 4,800.00	
15	Utilities Expense	6,720.00			
16	Totals	682,320.00	682,320.00	28,800.00	28,800.00
17	Net Income				

Name

CRITICAL THINKING PROBLEM 6.1 (continued)

ADJUSTED TRIAL BALANCE		INCOME STATEMENT		BALANCE SHEET		
DEBIT	CREDIT	DEBIT	CREDIT	DEBIT	CREDIT	
						1
						2
						3
						4
						5
						6
						7
						8
						9
						10
						11
						12
						13
						14
						15
						16
						17
						18
						19
						20
						21
						22
						23
						24
						25
						26
						27
						28
						29
						30
						31
						32

Name

CRITICAL THINKING PROBLEM 6.1 (continued)

Name ____________________

CRITICAL THINKING PROBLEM 6.1 (continued)

GENERAL JOURNAL

PAGE ________

	DATE		DESCRIPTION	POST. REF.	DEBIT	CREDIT	
1							1
2							2
3							3
4							4
5							5
6							6
7							7
8							8
9							9
10							10
11							11
12							12
13							13
14							14
15							15
16							16

Name

CRITICAL THINKING PROBLEM 6.1 (continued)

GENERAL JOURNAL

PAGE

	DATE		DESCRIPTION	POST. REF.	DEBIT	CREDIT	
1							1
2							2
3							3
4							4
5							5
6							6
7							7
8							8
9							9
10							10
11							11
12							12
13							13
14							14
15							15
16							16
17							17
18							18

ACCOUNT NAME	DEBIT	CREDIT

Analyze:

Name

CRITICAL THINKING PROBLEM 6.2

1.

2.

GENERAL JOURNAL PAGE ____

	DATE		DESCRIPTION	POST. REF.	DEBIT	CREDIT	
1							1
2							2
3							3
4							4
5							5
6							6

3.

Name

CRITICAL THINKING PROBLEM 6.2 (continued)

Chapter 6 Practice Test Answer Key

Part A True-False

1. T
2. F
3. F
4. T
5. F
6. T
7. F
8. T
9. F
10. F

Part B Matching

1. a
2. b
3. c
4. e
5. d

MINI-PRACTICE SET 1

Name

Service Business Accounting Cycle

GENERAL JOURNAL

PAGE

DATE	DESCRIPTION	POST. REF.	DEBIT	CREDIT

 Name

GENERAL JOURNAL

PAGE

DATE	DESCRIPTION	POST. REF.	DEBIT	CREDIT

 Name

GENERAL JOURNAL

PAGE

DATE	DESCRIPTION	POST. REF.	DEBIT	CREDIT

 Name ______________

GENERAL JOURNAL

PAGE ______

DATE	DESCRIPTION	POST. REF.	DEBIT	CREDIT

 Name

GENERAL LEDGER

ACCOUNT ______ ACCOUNT NO. ______

DATE	DESCRIPTION	POST. REF.	DEBIT	CREDIT	BALANCE	
					DEBIT	CREDIT

ACCOUNT ______ ACCOUNT NO. ______

DATE	DESCRIPTION	POST. REF.	DEBIT	CREDIT	BALANCE	
					DEBIT	CREDIT

 Name

GENERAL LEDGER

ACCOUNT ACCOUNT NO.

DATE	DESCRIPTION	POST. REF.	DEBIT	CREDIT	BALANCE DEBIT	BALANCE CREDIT

ACCOUNT ACCOUNT NO.

DATE	DESCRIPTION	POST. REF.	DEBIT	CREDIT	BALANCE DEBIT	BALANCE CREDIT

ACCOUNT ACCOUNT NO.

DATE	DESCRIPTION	POST. REF.	DEBIT	CREDIT	BALANCE DEBIT	BALANCE CREDIT

ACCOUNT ACCOUNT NO.

DATE	DESCRIPTION	POST. REF.	DEBIT	CREDIT	BALANCE DEBIT	BALANCE CREDIT

ACCOUNT ACCOUNT NO.

DATE	DESCRIPTION	POST. REF.	DEBIT	CREDIT	BALANCE DEBIT	BALANCE CREDIT

 Name ____________

GENERAL LEDGER

ACCOUNT ____________ ACCOUNT NO. ____

DATE	DESCRIPTION	POST. REF.	DEBIT	CREDIT	BALANCE DEBIT	BALANCE CREDIT

ACCOUNT ____________ ACCOUNT NO. ____

DATE	DESCRIPTION	POST. REF.	DEBIT	CREDIT	BALANCE DEBIT	BALANCE CREDIT

ACCOUNT ____________ ACCOUNT NO. ____

DATE	DESCRIPTION	POST. REF.	DEBIT	CREDIT	BALANCE DEBIT	BALANCE CREDIT

ACCOUNT ____________ ACCOUNT NO. ____

DATE	DESCRIPTION	POST. REF.	DEBIT	CREDIT	BALANCE DEBIT	BALANCE CREDIT

 Name

GENERAL LEDGER

ACCOUNT ______ ACCOUNT NO. ______

DATE		DESCRIPTION	POST. REF.	DEBIT	CREDIT	BALANCE	
						DEBIT	CREDIT

ACCOUNT ______ ACCOUNT NO. ______

DATE		DESCRIPTION	POST. REF.	DEBIT	CREDIT	BALANCE	
						DEBIT	CREDIT

ACCOUNT ______ ACCOUNT NO. ______

DATE		DESCRIPTION	POST. REF.	DEBIT	CREDIT	BALANCE	
						DEBIT	CREDIT

ACCOUNT ______ ACCOUNT NO. ______

DATE		DESCRIPTION	POST. REF.	DEBIT	CREDIT	BALANCE	
						DEBIT	CREDIT

ACCOUNT ______ ACCOUNT NO. ______

DATE		DESCRIPTION	POST. REF.	DEBIT	CREDIT	BALANCE	
						DEBIT	CREDIT

 Name ____________

GENERAL LEDGER

ACCOUNT ____________ ACCOUNT NO. ______

DATE		DESCRIPTION	POST. REF.	DEBIT	CREDIT	BALANCE DEBIT	BALANCE CREDIT

ACCOUNT ____________ ACCOUNT NO. ______

DATE		DESCRIPTION	POST. REF.	DEBIT	CREDIT	BALANCE DEBIT	BALANCE CREDIT

ACCOUNT ____________ ACCOUNT NO. ______

DATE		DESCRIPTION	POST. REF.	DEBIT	CREDIT	BALANCE DEBIT	BALANCE CREDIT

ACCOUNT ____________ ACCOUNT NO. ______

DATE		DESCRIPTION	POST. REF.	DEBIT	CREDIT	BALANCE DEBIT	BALANCE CREDIT

ACCOUNT ____________ ACCOUNT NO. ______

DATE		DESCRIPTION	POST. REF.	DEBIT	CREDIT	BALANCE DEBIT	BALANCE CREDIT

 Name

ACCOUNT NAME	TRIAL BALANCE		ADJUSTMENTS	
	DEBIT	CREDIT	DEBIT	CREDIT

 Name ______________________

ADJUSTED TRIAL BALANCE		INCOME STATEMENT		BALANCE SHEET		
DEBIT	CREDIT	DEBIT	CREDIT	DEBIT	CREDIT	
						1
						2
						3
						4
						5
						6
						7
						8
						9
						10
						11
						12
						13
						14
						15
						16
						17
						18
						19
						20
						21
						22
						23
						24
						25
						26
						27
						28
						29
						30
						31
						32
						33
						34
						35
						36
						37

 Name

 Name

ACCOUNT NAME	DEBIT	CREDIT

 Name

Analyze:

CHAPTER 7

Accounting for Sales and Accounts Receivable

STUDY GUIDE

Understanding the Chapter

Objectives — **1.** Record credit sales in a sales journal. **2.** Post from the sales journal to the general ledger accounts. **3.** Post from the sales journal to the customers' accounts in the accounts receivable subsidiary ledger. **4.** Record sales returns and allowances in the general journal. **5.** Post sales returns and allowances. **6.** Prepare a schedule of accounts receivable. **7.** Compute trade discounts. **8.** Record credit card sales in appropriate journals. **9.** Prepare the state sales tax return. **10.** Define the accounting terms new to this chapter.

Reading Assignment — Read Chapter 7 in the textbook. Complete the textbook Section Self Review as you finish reading each section of the chapter, and the Comprehensive Self Review at the end of the chapter. Refer to the Chapter 7 Glossary or to the Glossary at the end of the book to find definitions for terms that are not familiar to you.

Activities

- ❑ **Thinking Critically** — Answer the *Thinking Critically* questions for indi and Managerial Implications.
- ❑ **Discussion Questions** — Answer each assigned discussion question in Chapter 7.
- ❑ **Exercises** — Complete each assigned exercise in Chapter 7. Use the forms provided in this SGWP. The objectives covered by an exercise are given after the exercise number. If you need help with an exercise, review the portion of the chapter related to the objective(s) covered.
- ❑ **Problems A/B** — Complete each assigned problem in Chapter 7. Use the forms provided in this SGWP. The objectives covered by a problem are given after the problem number. If you need help with a problem, review the portion of the chapter related to the objective(s) covered.
- ❑ **Critical Thinking Problems** — Complete the critical thinking problems 7.1 and 7.2 as assigned. Use the forms provided in this SGWP.
- ❑ **Business Connections** — Complete the Business Connections activities as assigned to gain a deeper understanding of Chapter 7 concepts.

Practice Tests

Complete the Practice Tests, which cover the main points in your reading assignment. Compare your answers with those in the Practice Test Answer Key for Chapter 7 at the end of this chapter. If you have answered any questions incorrectly, review the related section of the text.

Part A True-False *For each of the following statements, circle T in the answer column if the statement is true and F if the statement is false.*

T F **1.** The accountant must keep an individual record of dealings with each customer to answer questions received from managers and salespeople of the company, from the customers themselves, and from banks and credit bureaus.

T F **2.** A credit sale made on a credit card issued by a credit card company is accounted for in the same manner as a credit sale made on a bank credit card.

T F **3.** The **Accounts Receivable** account in the general ledger is known as a control account because it contains a summary of all activities involving accounts receivable.

T F **4.** As proof of accuracy, the total of all customers' accounts in the accounts receivable ledger is compared with the balance of the **Accounts Receivable** account in the general ledger.

T F **5.** The basic procedure for posting totals from the sales journal to the general ledger is not affected by the use of an accounts receivable ledger.

T F **6.** When the balance-form ledger sheet is used in the accounts receivable ledger, the accountant figures the running balance of each account after each posting during the month.

T F **7.** The accounts receivable ledger is called a subsidiary ledger because it is only a part of the general ledger.

T F **8.** The amount of each credit sale is posted daily to the customer's account in the accounts receivable ledger.

T F **9.** When a customer returns goods on which sales tax was charged, the firm gives credit for the price of goods but not the sales tax.

T F **10.** The **Accounts Receivable** account in the general ledger must be individually debited for each credit sale as it is made.

T F **11.** The larger the volume of credit sales, the more desirable it is to use a special sales journal.

T F **12.** The amount of a sales allowance is debited to the Sales account because the revenue from sales has been reduced.

T F **13.** The Sales Slip Number column in the sales journal shows where to look when more information is needed.

T F **14.** The use of a special sales journal enables more than one person to work on the journals of a business at the same time.

T F **15.** Special journals are needed when the transactions of a business include groups of repetitive entries.

T F **16.** Sales on credit require debits to **Accounts Payable.**

T F **17.** The Sales account may be credited for a sale made for cash but not on account.

T F **18.** The special sales journal is used for recording both cash sales and sales on credit.

T F **19.** The columns and headings in the sales journal eliminate the need for a description of each entity.

T F **20.** The use of a special sales journal makes posting individual sales transactions to accounts in the general ledger unnecessary.

Part B Matching *For each numbered item, choose the matching term from the box and write the identifying letter in the answer column.*

a. Trade discount
b. Sales return or allowance
c. Business credit card
d. Sales tax payable
e. Open-account credit
f. Sales journal
g. Bank credit cards

_______ **1.** A reduction in the amount charged to a customer who has received defective goods or services.

_______ **2.** A liability account for recording a tax levied by some states on certain retail sales.

_______ **3.** A special journal for recording only the credit sales of a company.

_______ **4.** Identification cards used by some banks to individuals for use in making credit card purchases at participating businesses.

_______ **5.** Identification cards given by some businesses to their customers who have established credit.

_______ **6.** The type of credit usually given by a business on the basis of the personal knowledge of the customer.

_______ **7.** A reduction in price, based on volume purchased, given by wholesalers to retailers who buy goods for resale.

Part C Exercise *Answer each question about the accounts receivable subsidiary ledger account shown below.*

ACCOUNTS RECEIVABLE SUBSIDIARY LEDGER

NAME **Charles Kronos** TERMS _______

ADDRESS **1891 Windsor Drive, Dallas, TX 75623-6998**

DATE		DESCRIPTION	POST. REF.	DEBIT	CREDIT	BALANCE DEBIT	BALANCE CREDIT
2013							
Jan.	**1**	**Balance**	✔			**400 00**	
	4	**Sales Slip 101**	**S1**	**60 00**		**460 00**	
	7	**Sales Slip 167**	**S1**	**90 00**		**550 00**	
	18		**J1**		**80 00**	**470 00**	

1. Where did the $400 entry come from?

____

____

2. How could you find a complete description of the $60 charge on January 4?

____

____

3. What was the probable reason for the $80.00 entry? How can you find out for sure?

____

____

Demonstration Problem

Coastal Auto Supply sells tires and auto supplies to retail stores. The firm offers a trade discount of 40 percent on tires and 20 percent on auto supplies. Transactions involving credit sales and sales returns and allowances for the month of April 2013 follow, along with the general ledger accounts used to record these transactions. Account balances shown are for the beginning of April 2013.

Instructions

1. Open the general ledger accounts; enter the balance for **Accounts Receivable.**

111	Accounts Receivable $61,020
401	Sales
451	Sales Returns and Allowances

2. Set up the accounts receivable subsidiary ledger. Open an account for each credit customer and enter the balances as of April 1, 2013. All customers have terms of n/45.

Auto Warehouse	$ —
Dave's Auto Mart	$14,790
Jazzy Wheels and Window Tint Center	$42,000
Mike's Car Care Center	$4,230
Paso Auto Express	$ —

3. Record the transactions on page 6 of a sales journal and on page 16 of the general journal. (Be sure to enter each sale at its net price.)
4. Post individual entries from the sales journal and the general journal to the appropriate ledger accounts.
5. Total and rule the sales journal as of April 30, 2013.
6. Post from the sales journal to the appropriate general ledger accounts.
7. Prepare a schedule of accounts receivable for April 30, 2013.
8. Compare the total of the schedule of accounts receivable to the balance of the **Accounts Receivable** account. The two should be equal.

DATE	TRANSACTIONS
April 1	Sold tires to Auto Warehouse; issued sales slip 6701 with a list price of $50,000.
5	Sold auto supplies to Mike's Car Care Center; issued sales slip 6702 with a list price of $50,200.
9	Sold auto supplies to Jazzy Wheels and Window Tint Center; issued sales slip 6703 with a list price of $19,800.
14	Sold tires to Dave's Auto Mart, issued sales slip 6704 with a list price of $49,200.
18	Accepted a return of all auto supplies damaged in shipment to Jazzy Wheels and Window Tint Center; issued Credit Memorandum 251. The original sale was made on sales slip 6703 on April 9.
22	Sold auto supplies to Auto Warehouse; issued sales slip 6705 with a list price of $83,480.
29	Sold tires to Mike's Car Care Center; issued sales slip 6706 with a list price of $87,230.
30	Sold tires to Paso Auto Express; issued sales slip 6707 with a list price of $43,230.

SOLUTION

SALES JOURNAL

PAGE 6

DATE		INVOICE NO.	CUSTOMER'S NAME	POST. REF.	ACCOUNTS RECEIVABLE/ DR. SALES CR.
2013					
April	1	6701	Auto Warehouse	✔	30 0 0 0 00
	5	6702	Mike's Car Care Center	✔	40 1 6 0 00
	9	6703	Jazzy Wheels and Window Tint Center	✔	15 8 4 0 00
	14	6704	Dave's Auto Mart	✔	29 5 2 0 00
	22	6705	Auto Warehouse	✔	66 7 8 4 00
	29	6706	Mike's Car Care Center	✔	52 3 3 8 00
	30	6707	Paso Auto Express	✔	25 9 3 8 00
			Totals		260 5 8 0 00
					(1 1 1/4 0 1)

GENERAL JOURNAL

PAGE 16

DATE		DESCRIPTION	POST. REF.	DEBIT	CREDIT
2013					
April	18	Sales Returns and Allowances	451	15 8 4 0 00	
		Accounts Rec./Jazzy Wheels	111/✔		15 8 4 0 00
		and Window Tint Center			
		Accepted return of damaged supplies,			
		Credit Memo 251; original sale			
		made on Invoice 6703 of April 9			

GENERAL LEDGER

ACCOUNT **Accounts Receivable** ACCOUNT NO. **111**

DATE		DESCRIPTION	POST. REF.	DEBIT	CREDIT	BALANCE DEBIT	BALANCE CREDIT
2013							
April	1	Balance	✔			61 0 2 0 00	
	18		J16		15 8 4 0 00	45 1 8 0 00	
	30		S6	260 5 8 0 00		305 7 6 0 00	

SOLUTION (continued)

GENERAL LEDGER

ACCOUNT **Sales** ACCOUNT NO. **401**

DATE		DESCRIPTION	POST. REF.	DEBIT	CREDIT	BALANCE DEBIT	BALANCE CREDIT
2013							
April	**30**		**S6**		**260 5 8 0 00**		**260 5 8 0 00**

ACCOUNT **Sales Returns and Allowances** ACCOUNT NO. **451**

DATE		DESCRIPTION	POST. REF.	DEBIT	CREDIT	BALANCE DEBIT	BALANCE CREDIT
2013							
April	**18**		**J16**	**15 8 4 0 00**		**15 8 4 0 00**	

ACCOUNTS RECEIVABLE SUBSIDIARY LEDGER

NAME **Auto Warehouse** TERMS **n/45**

DATE		DESCRIPTION	POST. REF.	DEBIT	CREDIT	BALANCE DEBIT	BALANCE CREDIT
2013							
April	**1**	**Sales Slip 6701**	**S6**	**30 0 0 0 00**		**30 0 0 0 00**	
	22	**Sales Slip 6705**	**S6**	**66 7 8 4 00**		**96 7 8 4 00**	

NAME **Dave's Auto Mart** TERMS **n/45**

DATE		DESCRIPTION	POST. REF.	DEBIT	CREDIT	BALANCE DEBIT	BALANCE CREDIT
2013							
April	**1**	**Balance**	✔			**14 7 9 0 00**	
	14	**Sales Slip 6704**	**S6**	**29 5 2 0 00**		**44 3 1 0 00**	

SOLUTION (continued)

ACCOUNTS RECEIVABLE SUBSIDIARY LEDGER

NAME **Jazzy Wheels and Window Tint Center** TERMS **n/45**

DATE		DESCRIPTION	POST. REF.	DEBIT	CREDIT	BALANCE DEBIT	BALANCE CREDIT
2013							
April	**1**	**Balance**	✔			**42,000.00**	
	9	**Sales Slip 6703**	**S6**	**15,840.00**		**57,840.00**	
	18	**CM 251**	**J16**		**15,840.00**	**42,000.00**	

NAME **Mike's Car Care Center** TERMS **n/45**

DATE		DESCRIPTION	POST. REF.	DEBIT	CREDIT	BALANCE DEBIT	BALANCE CREDIT
2013							
April	**1**	**Balance**	✔			**4,230.00**	
	5	**Sales Slip 6702**	**S6**	**40,160.00**		**44,390.00**	
	29	**Sales Slip 6706**	**S6**	**52,338.00**		**96,728.00**	

NAME **Paso Auto Express** TERMS **n/45**

DATE		DESCRIPTION	POST. REF.	DEBIT	CREDIT	BALANCE DEBIT	BALANCE CREDIT
2013							
April	**30**	**Sales Slip 6707**	**S6**	**25,938.00**		**25,938.00**	

Coastal Auto Supply

Schedule of Accounts Receivable

April 30, 2013

Auto Warehouse	**96,784.00**
Dave's Auto Mart	**44,310.00**
Jazzy Wheels and Window Tint Center	**42,000.00**
Mike's Car Care Center	**96,728.00**
Paso Auto Express	**25,938.00**
Total	**305,760.00**

WORKING PAPERS

Name ______________________

EXERCISE 7.1

1. ______________________
2. ______________________
3. ______________________
4. ______________________
5. ______________________
6. ______________________
7. ______________________
8. ______________________

EXERCISE 7.2

	Dr.	Cr.		Dr.	Cr.
1.			4.		
2.			5.		
3.			6.		

EXERCISE 7.3

SALES JOURNAL PAGE ______

	DATE	SALES SLIP NO.	CUSTOMER'S NAME	POST. REF.	ACCOUNTS RECEIVABLE DEBIT	SALES TAX PAYABLE CREDIT	SALES CREDIT	
1								1
2								2
3								3
4								4
5								5

Name ____________________

EXERCISE 7.4

GENERAL JOURNAL PAGE ______

DATE		DESCRIPTION	POST. REF.	DEBIT	CREDIT

EXERCISE 7.5

1. ____________________

2. ____________________

3. ____________________

4. ____________________

EXERCISE 7.6

1. ____________________
2. ____________________
3. ____________________

Name ____________________

EXERCISE 7.7

1. ____________________
2. ____________________
3. ____________________

EXERCISE 7.8

GENERAL JOURNAL

PAGE ______

	DATE	DESCRIPTION	POST. REF.	DEBIT	CREDIT	
1						1
2						2
3						3
4						4
5						5

EXERCISE 7.9

Balance of Accounts Receivable: ____________

Name

EXERCISE 7.10

GENERAL LEDGER

ACCOUNT ______ ACCOUNT NO. ______

DATE		DESCRIPTION	POST. REF.	DEBIT	CREDIT	BALANCE	
						DEBIT	CREDIT

ACCOUNT ______ ACCOUNT NO. ______

DATE		DESCRIPTION	POST. REF.	DEBIT	CREDIT	BALANCE	
						DEBIT	CREDIT

ACCOUNT ______ ACCOUNT NO. ______

DATE		DESCRIPTION	POST. REF.	DEBIT	CREDIT	BALANCE	
						DEBIT	CREDIT

ACCOUNTS RECEIVABLE SUBSIDIARY LEDGER

NAME ______ TERMS ______

DATE		DESCRIPTION	POST. REF.	DEBIT	CREDIT	BALANCE

NAME ______ TERMS ______

DATE		DESCRIPTION	POST. REF.	DEBIT	CREDIT	BALANCE

Name ______________________________

PROBLEM 7.1A or 7.1B

SALES JOURNAL

PAGE ______

	DATE	SALES SLIP NO.	CUSTOMER'S NAME	POST. REF.	ACCOUNTS RECEIVABLE DEBIT	SALES TAX PAYABLE CREDIT	SALES CREDIT	
1								1
2								2
3								3
4								4
5								5
6								6
7								7
8								8
9								9
10								10
11								11
12								12

GENERAL LEDGER

ACCOUNT ______________________ ACCOUNT NO. ______

DATE	DESCRIPTION	POST. REF.	DEBIT	CREDIT	BALANCE	
					DEBIT	CREDIT

ACCOUNT ______________________ ACCOUNT NO. ______

DATE	DESCRIPTION	POST. REF.	DEBIT	CREDIT	BALANCE	
					DEBIT	CREDIT

ACCOUNT ______________________ ACCOUNT NO. ______

DATE	DESCRIPTION	POST. REF.	DEBIT	CREDIT	BALANCE	
					DEBIT	CREDIT

Analyze: ______________________________

Name ______________________

PROBLEM 7.2A or 7.2B

SALES JOURNAL

PAGE ______

DATE	SALES SLIP NO.	CUSTOMER'S NAME	POST. REF.	ACCOUNTS RECEIVABLE DEBIT	SALES TAX PAYABLE CREDIT	SALES CREDIT

GENERAL JOURNAL

PAGE ______

DATE	DESCRIPTION	POST. REF.	DEBIT	CREDIT

Name

PROBLEM 7.2A or 7.2B (continued)

GENERAL LEDGER

ACCOUNT ______ ACCOUNT NO. ______

DATE	DESCRIPTION	POST. REF.	DEBIT	CREDIT	BALANCE DEBIT	BALANCE CREDIT

ACCOUNT ______ ACCOUNT NO. ______

DATE	DESCRIPTION	POST. REF.	DEBIT	CREDIT	BALANCE DEBIT	BALANCE CREDIT

ACCOUNT ______ ACCOUNT NO. ______

DATE	DESCRIPTION	POST. REF.	DEBIT	CREDIT	BALANCE DEBIT	BALANCE CREDIT

ACCOUNT ______ ACCOUNT NO. ______

DATE	DESCRIPTION	POST. REF.	DEBIT	CREDIT	BALANCE DEBIT	BALANCE CREDIT

Name

PROBLEM 7.2A or 7.2B (continued)

Analyze:

PROBLEM 7.3A or 7.3B

SALES JOURNAL PAGE

	DATE		SALES SLIP NO.	CUSTOMER'S NAME	POST. REF.	ACCOUNTS RECEIVABLE DEBIT	SALES TAX PAYABLE CREDIT	SALES CREDIT	
1									1
2									2
3									3
4									4
5									5
6									6
7									7
8									8
9									9
10									10
11									11
12									12

Name

PROBLEM 7.3A or 7.3B (continued)

GENERAL JOURNAL

PAGE

	DATE		DESCRIPTION	POST. REF.	DEBIT	CREDIT	
1							1
2							2
3							3
4							4
5							5
6							6
7							7
8							8
9							9
10							10
11							11
12							12
13							13
14							14
15							15

GENERAL LEDGER

ACCOUNT ACCOUNT NO.

DATE		DESCRIPTION	POST. REF.	DEBIT	CREDIT	BALANCE	
						DEBIT	CREDIT

ACCOUNT ACCOUNT NO.

DATE		DESCRIPTION	POST. REF.	DEBIT	CREDIT	BALANCE	
						DEBIT	CREDIT

Name ____________________

PROBLEM 7.3A or 7.3B (continued)

GENERAL LEDGER

ACCOUNT ____________________ ACCOUNT NO. ________

DATE		DESCRIPTION	POST. REF.	DEBIT	CREDIT	BALANCE DEBIT	BALANCE CREDIT

ACCOUNT ____________________ ACCOUNT NO. ________

DATE		DESCRIPTION	POST. REF.	DEBIT	CREDIT	BALANCE DEBIT	BALANCE CREDIT

ACCOUNTS RECEIVABLE SUBSIDIARY LEDGER

NAME ____________________ TERMS ________

DATE		DESCRIPTION	POST. REF.	DEBIT	CREDIT	BALANCE

NAME ____________________ TERMS ________

DATE		DESCRIPTION	POST. REF.	DEBIT	CREDIT	BALANCE

NAME ____________________ TERMS ________

DATE		DESCRIPTION	POST. REF.	DEBIT	CREDIT	BALANCE

Name

PROBLEM 7.3A or 7.3B (continued)

ACCOUNTS RECEIVABLE SUBSIDIARY LEDGER

NAME ______________________ TERMS ______

DATE		DESCRIPTION	POST. REF.	DEBIT	CREDIT	BALANCE

NAME ______________________ TERMS ______

DATE		DESCRIPTION	POST. REF.	DEBIT	CREDIT	BALANCE

NAME ______________________ TERMS ______

DATE		DESCRIPTION	POST. REF.	DEBIT	CREDIT	BALANCE

NAME ______________________ TERMS ______

DATE		DESCRIPTION	POST. REF.	DEBIT	CREDIT	BALANCE

NAME ______________________ TERMS ______

DATE		DESCRIPTION	POST. REF.	DEBIT	CREDIT	BALANCE

NAME ______________________ TERMS ______

DATE		DESCRIPTION	POST. REF.	DEBIT	CREDIT	BALANCE

Name ____________________

PROBLEM 7.3A or 7.3B (continued)

Balance of Accounts Receivable account: ____________

Analyze: ____________________

PROBLEM 7.4A or 7.4B

SALES JOURNAL PAGE ____

	DATE		SALES SLIP NO.	CUSTOMER'S NAME	POST. REF.	ACCOUNTS RECEIVABLE DR./ SALES CR.	
1							1
2							2
3							3
4							4
5							5
6							6
7							7
8							8
9							9
10							10
11							11
12							12

Name

PROBLEM 7.4A or 7.4B (continued)

GENERAL JOURNAL

PAGE

	DATE		DESCRIPTION	POST. REF.	DEBIT	CREDIT	
1							1
2							2
3							3
4							4
5							5
6							6
7							7
8							8
9							9
10							10
11							11
12							12
13							13

GENERAL LEDGER

ACCOUNT ACCOUNT NO.

DATE		DESCRIPTION	POST. REF.	DEBIT	CREDIT	BALANCE	
						DEBIT	CREDIT

ACCOUNT ACCOUNT NO.

DATE		DESCRIPTION	POST. REF.	DEBIT	CREDIT	BALANCE	
						DEBIT	CREDIT

ACCOUNT ACCOUNT NO.

DATE		DESCRIPTION	POST. REF.	DEBIT	CREDIT	BALANCE	
						DEBIT	CREDIT

Name

PROBLEM 7.4A or 7.4B (continued)

ACCOUNTS RECEIVABLE SUBSIDIARY LEDGER

NAME TERMS

DATE		DESCRIPTION	POST. REF.	DEBIT	CREDIT	BALANCE

NAME TERMS

DATE		DESCRIPTION	POST. REF.	DEBIT	CREDIT	BALANCE

NAME TERMS

DATE		DESCRIPTION	POST. REF.	DEBIT	CREDIT	BALANCE

NAME TERMS

DATE		DESCRIPTION	POST. REF.	DEBIT	CREDIT	BALANCE

NAME TERMS

DATE		DESCRIPTION	POST. REF.	DEBIT	CREDIT	BALANCE

Name

PROBLEM 7.4A or 7.4B (continued)

ACCOUNTS RECEIVABLE SUBSIDIARY LEDGER

NAME ____________ TERMS ____________

DATE		DESCRIPTION	POST. REF.	DEBIT	CREDIT	BALANCE

Balance of Accounts Receivable account: ________

Analyze: ________

CRITICAL THINKING PROBLEM 7.1

SALES JOURNAL

PAGE ________

	DATE		SALES SLIP NO.	CUSTOMER'S NAME	POST. REF.	ACCOUNTS RECEIVABLE DR./ SALES CR.	
1							1
2							2
3							3
4							4
5							5
6							6
7							7
8							8
9							9
10							10
11							11

Name ____________________

CRITICAL THINKING PROBLEM 7.1 (continued)

GENERAL JOURNAL

PAGE ______

	DATE		DESCRIPTION	POST. REF.	DEBIT	CREDIT	
1							1
2							2
3							3
4							4
5							5
6							6
7							7

GENERAL LEDGER

ACCOUNT ____________________ ACCOUNT NO. ______

DATE		DESCRIPTION	POST. REF.	DEBIT	CREDIT	BALANCE	
						DEBIT	CREDIT

ACCOUNT ____________________ ACCOUNT NO. ______

DATE		DESCRIPTION	POST. REF.	DEBIT	CREDIT	BALANCE	
						DEBIT	CREDIT

ACCOUNT ____________________ ACCOUNT NO. ______

DATE		DESCRIPTION	POST. REF.	DEBIT	CREDIT	BALANCE	
						DEBIT	CREDIT

Name

CRITICAL THINKING PROBLEM 7.1 (continued)

ACCOUNTS RECEIVABLE LEDGER

NAME ______ TERMS ______

DATE		DESCRIPTION	POST. REF.	DEBIT	CREDIT	BALANCE

NAME ______ TERMS ______

DATE		DESCRIPTION	POST. REF.	DEBIT	CREDIT	BALANCE

NAME ______ TERMS ______

DATE		DESCRIPTION	POST. REF.	DEBIT	CREDIT	BALANCE

NAME ______ TERMS ______

DATE		DESCRIPTION	POST. REF.	DEBIT	CREDIT	BALANCE

NAME ______ TERMS ______

DATE		DESCRIPTION	POST. REF.	DEBIT	CREDIT	BALANCE

Name ____________

CRITICAL THINKING PROBLEM 7.1 (continued)

ACCOUNTS RECEIVABLE SUBSIDIARY LEDGER

NAME ____________ TERMS ____________

DATE		DESCRIPTION	POST. REF.	DEBIT	CREDIT	BALANCE

Balance of Accounts Receivable account: ____________

Analyze: ____________

Name

CRITICAL THINKING PROBLEM 7.2

1.

2.

3.

4.

Chapter 7 Practice Test Answer Key

Part A True-False

1. T	11. T
2. F	12. F
3. T	13. T
4. T	14. T
5. T	15. T
6. T	16. F
7. F	17. F
8. T	18. F
9. F	19. T
10. F	20. T

Part B Matching

1. b
2. d
3. f
4. g
5. c
6. e
7. a

Part C Exercises

1. The balance was carried over from December 2012.
2. By referring to a copy of Sales Slip 101.
3. It was most likely a sales return or allowance. Refer to the January 18 entry on page 1 of the general journal.

CHAPTER 8

Accounting for Purchases and Accounts Payable

STUDY GUIDE

Understanding the Chapter

Objectives

1. Record purchases of merchandise on credit in a three-column purchases journal. **2.** Post from the three-column purchases journal to the general ledger accounts. **3.** Post credit purchases from the purchases journal to the accounts payable subsidiary ledger. **4.** Record purchases returns and allowances in the general journal and post them to the accounts payable subsidiary ledger. **5.** Prepare a schedule of accounts payable. **6.** Compute the net delivered cost of purchases. **7.** Demonstrate a knowledge of the procedures for effective internal control of purchases. **8.** Define the accounting terms new to this chapter.

Reading Assignment

Read Chapter 8 in the textbook. Complete the textbook Section Self Review as you finish reading each section of the chapter, and the Comprehensive Self Review at the end of the chapter. Refer to the Chapter 8 Glossary or to the Glossary at the end of the book to find definitions for terms that are not familiar to you.

Activities

- ❑ **Thinking Critically** — Answer the *Thinking Critically* questions for Williams Sonoma and Managerial Implications.
- ❑ **Discussion Questions** — Answer each assigned discussion question in Chapter 8.
- ❑ **Exercises** — Complete each assigned exercise in Chapter 8. Use the forms provided in this SGWP. The objectives covered by an exercise are given after the exercise number. If you need help with an exercise, review the portion of the chapter related to the objective(s) covered.
- ❑ **Problems A/B** — Complete each assigned problem in Chapter 8. Use the forms provided in this SGWP. The objectives covered by a problem are given after the problem number. If you need help with a problem, review the portion of the chapter related to the objective(s) covered.
- ❑ **Critical Thinking Problems** — Complete the critical thinking problems as assigned. Use the forms provided in this SGWP.
- ❑ **Business Connections** — Complete the Business Connections activities as assigned to gain a deeper understanding of Chapter 8 concepts.

Practice Tests

Complete the Practice Tests, which cover the main points in your reading assignment. Compare your answers with those in the Practice Test Answer Key for Chapter 8 at the end of this chapter. If you have answered any questions incorrectly, review the related section of the text.

Part A True-False *For each of the following statements, circle T in the answer column if the statement is true or F if the statement is false.*

T F 1. The special purchases journal is used to record all transactions in which merchandise or equipment is purchased on credit.

T F 2. A receiving report is prepared to show the quantity of goods received and their condition.

T F 3. Freight In becomes part of the cost of purchases shown in the Cost of Goods Sold section of the income statement.

T F 4. The procedure for posting totals from the purchases journal remains the same, whether or not an accounts payable ledger is used.

T F 5. A payment is first recorded in the cash payments journal and then debited immediately to the supplier's account in the accounts payable ledger.

T F 6. As soon as it is recorded in the **Purchases** journal, the amount of a purchase is posted as a credit to the supplier's account in the accounts payable ledger.

T F 7. After all postings for a period are completed, the total of the individual balances in the accounts payable ledger should be equal to the balance of the **Accounts Receivable** control account in the general ledger.

T F 8. Within the accounts payable ledger, the accounts for creditors are arranged alphabetically or by account number.

T F 9. The use of the balance ledger form makes each creditor's balance readily available.

T F 10. At the end of the month, the total of the payments made to creditors is debited to the **Accounts Payable** account.

T F 11. Returns of merchandise to suppliers are recorded in the general journal.

T F 12. Purchases Returns and Allowances is a contra-revenue account.

T F 13. Payments made to creditors are recorded in the cash payments journal.

T F 14. At the end of the month, the total of the Accounts Payable column in the purchases journal is debited to the **Accounts Payable** control account.

T F 15. The balance of each creditor's account in the accounts payable ledger is not computed until the end of the accounting period.

T F 16. Each purchase of merchandise on credit should be recorded in the purchases journal as it occurs during the month.

T F 17. One of the basic advantages of the purchases journal is that the posting to **Accounts Payable** is simplified.

T F 18. An account called **Purchases** is charged with the cost of the merchandise as it is sold.

T F 19. The provision in the purchases journal of special columns for the invoice number, the invoice date, and the credit terms is intended to ensure payment of the bill when it is due.

T F 20. When properly designed, a purchases journal makes posting to the general ledger unnecessary.

Part B Exercise *Answer each of the following in the space provided. Make your answers complete but as brief as possible.*

A firm uses a multicolumn purchases journal with the following money columns: Accounts Payable Credit, Purchases Debit, and Freight In Debit

1. How is the **Purchases** account classified?

2. How is the accuracy of the totals verified at the end of the month?

3. Which columns are totaled and summary posted to the general ledger?

4. If the buyer pays freight charges directly to the carrier on a purchase of merchandise, where is the freight transaction recorded?

5. The figures of which column are used to update the accounts payable ledger?

6. Where would you record the purchase of office equipment on open account credit terms?

7. Where is the **Freight In** account shown on the income statement?

Demonstration Problem

Santa Rosa Office Supply is a retail business that sells office equipment, furniture, and office supplies. Its credit purchases and purchases returns and allowances for the month of October 2013 follow. The general ledger accounts used to record these transactions are given below.

Instructions

1. Open the general ledger accounts and enter the balance of Accounts Payable for October 1, 2013.
2. Using the list of creditors that follows, open the accounts in the accounts payable subsidiary ledger and enter the account balances for October 1, 2013.
3. Record the transactions in a purchases journal, page 12, and a general journal, page 30.
4. Post individual entries from the purchases journal to the accounts payable subsidiary ledger, then post from the general journal to the general ledger and accounts payable subsidiary ledger.
5. Total, prove, and rule the purchases journal as of October 31, 2013.
6. Post the column totals from the purchases journal to the appropriate general ledger accounts.
7. Compute the net delivered cost of the firm's purchases for the month.
8. Prepare a schedule of accounts payable for October 31, 2013.
9. Check the total of the schedule of accounts payable against the balance of the **Accounts Payable** account in the general ledger. The two amounts should be equal.

GENERAL LEDGER ACCOUNTS

205 Accounts Payable	$18,900 Cr.
501 Purchases	
502 Freight In	
503 Purchases Returns and Allowances	

CREDITORS

Name	Terms	Balance
Bolanos Office Supplies	n/30	
Dallas Office Supply	n/60	$2,320
Davis Office Products	n/30	
Golden West Office Center	2/10, n/30	5,670
Trinh Copy and Paper	1/10, n/30	10,910

DATE	TRANSACTIONS
October 4	Purchased desks for $9,160 plus a freight charge of $280 from Davis Office Products, Invoice 3124 dated September 30, terms payable in 30 days.
9	Purchased computers for $7,450 from Bolanos Office Supplies, Invoice 7129 dated October 4, net due and payable in 30 days.
11	Received Credit Memo 165 for $600 from Davis Office Products as an allowance for slightly damaged but usable desks purchased on Invoice 3124 of September 30.
16	Purchased file cabinets for $2,720 plus a freight charge of $124 from Dallas Office Supply, Invoice 9088 dated October 11, terms of 60 days.
21	Purchased electronic calculators for $2,200 from Bolanos Office Supplies, Invoice 7765 dated October 16, net due and payable in 30 days.
24	Purchased laser printer paper for $3,350 plus a freight charge of $320 from Trinh Copy and Paper on Invoice 4891 dated October 19, terms of 1/10, n/30.
29	Received Credit Memo 629 for $540 from Bolanos Office Supplies for defective calculators that were returned. The calculators were originally purchased on Invoice 2765 of October 16.
31	Purchased office chairs for $4,300 plus a freight charge of $156 from Golden West Office Center, Invoice 966 dated October 26, terms of 2/10, n/30.

SOLUTION

PURCHASES JOURNAL

PAGE 12

DATE		CUSTOMER'S NAME	INVOICE NUMBER	INVOICE DATE	TERMS	POST. REF.	ACCOUNTS PAYABLE CREDIT	PURCHASES DEBIT	FREIGHT IN DEBIT
2013									
Oct.	4	Davis Office Products	3124	9/30	n/30		9440 00	9160 00	280 00
	9	Bolanos Office Supplies	7129	10/4	n/30		7450 00	7450 00	
	16	Dallas Office Supply	9088	10/11	n/60		2844 00	2720 00	124 00
	21	Bolanos Office Supplies	7765	10/16	n/30		2200 00	2200 00	
	24	Trinh Copy & Paper	4891	10/19	1/10, n/30		3670 00	3350 00	320 00
	31	Golden West Office Center	966	10/26	2/10, n/30		4456 00	4300 00	156 00
	31						30060 00	29180 00	880 00

GENERAL JOURNAL

PAGE 30

DATE		DESCRIPTION	POST. REF.	DEBIT	CREDIT
2013					
Oct.	11	Accounts Payable/Davis Office Products	205/✓	600 00	
		Purchases Returns and Allowances	503		600 00
		Received Credit Memo 165 for			
		damaged merchandise; original			
		purchase was made on Invoice 3124,			
		September 30, 2013			
	29	Accounts Payable/Bolanos Office Supplies	205/✓	540 00	
		Purchases Returns & Allowances	503		540 00
		Received Credit Memo 629 for damaged			
		merchandise that was returned;			
		original purchase was made on			
		Invoice 2765, October 16, 2013			

SOLUTION (continued)

GENERAL LEDGER

ACCOUNT **Accounts Payable** ACCOUNT NO. **205**

DATE		DESCRIPTION	POST. REF.	DEBIT	CREDIT	BALANCE DEBIT	BALANCE CREDIT
2013							
Oct.	**1**	**Balance**	✔				**18,900.00**
	11		**J30**	**600.00**			**18,300.00**
	29		**J30**	**540.00**			**17,760.00**
	31		**P12**		**30,060.00**		**47,820.00**

ACCOUNT **Purchases** ACCOUNT NO. **501**

DATE		DESCRIPTION	POST. REF.	DEBIT	CREDIT	BALANCE DEBIT	BALANCE CREDIT
2013							
Oct.	**31**		**P12**	**29,180.00**		**29,180.00**	

ACCOUNT **Freight In** ACCOUNT NO. **502**

DATE		DESCRIPTION	POST. REF.	DEBIT	CREDIT	BALANCE DEBIT	BALANCE CREDIT
2013							
Oct.	**31**		**P12**	**880.00**		**880.00**	

ACCOUNT **Purchases Returns and Allowances** ACCOUNT NO. **503**

DATE		DESCRIPTION	POST. REF.	DEBIT	CREDIT	BALANCE DEBIT	BALANCE CREDIT
2013							
Oct.	**11**		**J30**		**600.00**		**600.00**
	29		**J30**		**540.00**		**1,140.00**

Purchases	**$29,180**
Freight In	**880**
Delivered Cost of Purchases	**$30,060**
Less Purchases Returns and Allowances	**1,140**
Net Delivered Cost of Purchases	**$28,920**

SOLUTION (continued)

ACCOUNTS PAYABLE SUBSIDIARY LEDGER

NAME **Bolanos Office Supplies** TERMS **n/30**

DATE		DESCRIPTION	POST. REF.	DEBIT	CREDIT	BALANCE
2013						
Oct.	**9**	**Invoice 7129, 10/4/13**	**P12**		**7 4 5 0 00**	**7 4 5 0 00**
	21	**Invoice 7765, 10/16/13**	**P12**		**2 2 0 0 00**	**9 6 5 0 00**
	29	**CM 629**	**J30**	**5 4 0 00**		**9 1 1 0 00**

NAME **Dallas Office Supply** TERMS **n/60**

DATE		DESCRIPTION	POST. REF.	DEBIT	CREDIT	BALANCE
2013						
Oct.	**1**	**Balance**	✔			**2 3 2 0 00**
	16	**Invoice 9088, 10/11/13**	**P12**		**2 8 4 4 00**	**5 1 6 4 00**

NAME **Davis Office Products** TERMS **n/30**

DATE		DESCRIPTION	POST. REF.	DEBIT	CREDIT	BALANCE
2013						
Oct.	**4**	**Invoice 3124, 9/30/13**	**P12**		**9 4 4 0 00**	**9 4 4 0 00**
	11	**CM 165**	**J30**	**6 0 0 00**		**8 8 4 0 00**

NAME **Golden West Office Center** TERMS **2/10, n/30**

DATE		DESCRIPTION	POST. REF.	DEBIT	CREDIT	BALANCE
2013						
Oct.	**1**	**Balance**	✔			**5 6 7 0 00**
	31	**Invoice 966, 10/26/13**	**P12**		**4 4 5 6 00**	**10 1 2 6 00**

NAME **Trinh Copy and Paper** TERMS **1/10, n/30**

DATE		DESCRIPTION	POST. REF.	DEBIT	CREDIT	BALANCE
2013						
Oct.	**1**	**Balance**	✔			**10 9 1 0 00**
	24	**Invoice 4891, 10/19/13**	**P12**		**3 6 7 0 00**	**14 5 8 0 00**

SOLUTION (continued)

Santa Rosa Office Supply
Schedule of Accounts Payable
October 31, 2013

Bolanos Office Supplies	9,110.00
Dallas Office Supply	5,164.00
Davis Office Products	8,840.00
Golden West Office Center	10,126.00
Trinh Copy and Paper	14,580.00
Total	47,820.00

WORKING PAPERS

Name ______________________________

EXERCISE 8.1

1. ______________________ 4. ______________________
2. ______________________ 5. ______________________
3. ______________________ 6. ______________________

EXERCISE 8.2

	Dr.	Cr.		Dr.	Cr.
1.			4.		
2.			5.		
3.			6.		

EXERCISE 8.3

PURCHASES JOURNAL

PAGE ________

DATE		PURCHASED FROM	INVOICE NUMBER	INVOICE DATE	TERMS	POST. REF.	ACCOUNTS PAYABLE CREDIT	PURCHASES DEBIT	FREIGHT IN DEBIT

EXERCISE 8.4

GENERAL JOURNAL

PAGE ________

	DATE		DESCRIPTION	POST. REF.	DEBIT	CREDIT	
1							1
2							2
3							3
4							4
5							5
6							6
7							7
8							8
9							9
10							10

Name

EXERCISE 8.5

GENERAL JOURNAL PAGE

	DATE		DESCRIPTION	POST. REF.	DEBIT	CREDIT	
1							1
2							2
3							3
4							4
5							5
6							6
7							7

EXERCISE 8.6

EXERCISE 8.7

a.

b.

c.

d.

EXERCISE 8.8

a.

b.

c.

d.

Name

PROBLEM 8.1A or 8.1B

PURCHASES JOURNAL

PAGE

DATE	PURCHASED FROM	INVOICE NUMBER	INVOICE DATE	TERMS	POST. REF.	ACCOUNTS PAYABLE CREDIT	PURCHASES DEBIT	FREIGHT IN DEBIT

GENERAL JOURNAL

PAGE

DATE	DESCRIPTION	POST. REF.	DEBIT	CREDIT

Name ______________________

PROBLEM 8.1A or 8.1B (continued)

GENERAL LEDGER

ACCOUNT ______________________ ACCOUNT NO. ________

DATE		DESCRIPTION	POST. REF.	DEBIT	CREDIT	BALANCE DEBIT	BALANCE CREDIT

ACCOUNT ______________________ ACCOUNT NO. ________

DATE		DESCRIPTION	POST. REF.	DEBIT	CREDIT	BALANCE DEBIT	BALANCE CREDIT

ACCOUNT ______________________ ACCOUNT NO. ________

DATE		DESCRIPTION	POST. REF.	DEBIT	CREDIT	BALANCE DEBIT	BALANCE CREDIT

ACCOUNT ______________________ ACCOUNT NO. ________

DATE		DESCRIPTION	POST. REF.	DEBIT	CREDIT	BALANCE DEBIT	BALANCE CREDIT

Analyze: ______________________

Name ______________________

PROBLEM 8.2A or 8.2B

ACCOUNTS PAYABLE SUBSIDIARY LEDGER

NAME ______________________ TERMS ________

DATE	DESCRIPTION	POST. REF.	DEBIT	CREDIT	BALANCE

NAME ______________________ TERMS ________

DATE	DESCRIPTION	POST. REF.	DEBIT	CREDIT	BALANCE

NAME ______________________ TERMS ________

DATE	DESCRIPTION	POST. REF.	DEBIT	CREDIT	BALANCE

NAME ______________________ TERMS ________

DATE	DESCRIPTION	POST. REF.	DEBIT	CREDIT	BALANCE

NAME ______________________ TERMS ________

DATE	DESCRIPTION	POST. REF.	DEBIT	CREDIT	BALANCE

Name

PROBLEM 8.2A or 8.2B (continued)

Analyze:

EXTRA FORM

Name

PROBLEM 8.3A or 8.3B

PURCHASES JOURNAL

PAGE

DATE		PURCHASED FROM	INVOICE NUMBER	INVOICE DATE	TERMS	POST. REF.	ACCOUNTS PAYABLE CREDIT	PURCHASES DEBIT	FREIGHT IN DEBIT

GENERAL JOURNAL

PAGE

	DATE		DESCRIPTION	POST. REF.	DEBIT	CREDIT	
1							1
2							2
3							3
4							4
5							5
6							6
7							7
8							8
9							9
10							10
11							11
12							12
13							13
14							14
15							15

Name ______________________________

PROBLEM 8.3A or 8.3B (continued)

GENERAL LEDGER

ACCOUNT ______________________________ ACCOUNT NO. __________

DATE		DESCRIPTION	POST. REF.	DEBIT	CREDIT	BALANCE	
						DEBIT	CREDIT

ACCOUNT ______________________________ ACCOUNT NO. __________

DATE		DESCRIPTION	POST. REF.	DEBIT	CREDIT	BALANCE	
						DEBIT	CREDIT

ACCOUNT ______________________________ ACCOUNT NO. __________

DATE		DESCRIPTION	POST. REF.	DEBIT	CREDIT	BALANCE	
						DEBIT	CREDIT

ACCOUNT ______________________________ ACCOUNT NO. __________

DATE		DESCRIPTION	POST. REF.	DEBIT	CREDIT	BALANCE	
						DEBIT	CREDIT

Name

PROBLEM 8.3A or 8.3B (continued)

ACCOUNTS PAYABLE SUBSIDIARY LEDGER

NAME TERMS

DATE		DESCRIPTION	POST. REF.	DEBIT	CREDIT	BALANCE

NAME TERMS

DATE		DESCRIPTION	POST. REF.	DEBIT	CREDIT	BALANCE

NAME TERMS

DATE		DESCRIPTION	POST. REF.	DEBIT	CREDIT	BALANCE

NAME TERMS

DATE		DESCRIPTION	POST. REF.	DEBIT	CREDIT	BALANCE

NAME TERMS

DATE		DESCRIPTION	POST. REF.	DEBIT	CREDIT	BALANCE

Name

PROBLEM 8.3A or 8.3B (continued)

Analyze:

EXTRA FORMS

NAME TERMS

DATE		DESCRIPTION	POST. REF.	DEBIT	CREDIT	BALANCE

NAME TERMS

DATE		DESCRIPTION	POST. REF.	DEBIT	CREDIT	BALANCE

Name

PROBLEM 8.4A or 8.4B

PURCHASES JOURNAL

PAGE

DATE	PURCHASED FROM	INVOICE NUMBER	INVOICE DATE	TERMS	POST. REF.	ACCOUNTS PAYABLE CREDIT	PURCHASES DEBIT	FREIGHT IN DEBIT

GENERAL JOURNAL

PAGE

	DATE	DESCRIPTION	POST. REF.	DEBIT	CREDIT	
1						1
2						2
3						3
4						4
5						5
6						6
7						7
8						8
9						9
10						10
11						11
12						12
13						13
14						14
15						15

Name

PROBLEM 8.4A or 8.4B (continued)

GENERAL LEDGER

ACCOUNT ACCOUNT NO.

DATE		DESCRIPTION	POST. REF.	DEBIT	CREDIT	BALANCE	
						DEBIT	CREDIT

ACCOUNT ACCOUNT NO.

DATE		DESCRIPTION	POST. REF.	DEBIT	CREDIT	BALANCE	
						DEBIT	CREDIT

ACCOUNT ACCOUNT NO.

DATE		DESCRIPTION	POST. REF.	DEBIT	CREDIT	BALANCE	
						DEBIT	CREDIT

ACCOUNT ACCOUNT NO.

DATE		DESCRIPTION	POST. REF.	DEBIT	CREDIT	BALANCE	
						DEBIT	CREDIT

Net Delivered Cost of Purchases

Name ______________________

PROBLEM 8.4A or 8.4B (continued)

ACCOUNTS PAYABLE SUBSIDIARY LEDGER

NAME ______________________ TERMS ______

DATE		DESCRIPTION	POST. REF.	DEBIT	CREDIT	BALANCE

NAME ______________________ TERMS ______

DATE		DESCRIPTION	POST. REF.	DEBIT	CREDIT	BALANCE

NAME ______________________ TERMS ______

DATE		DESCRIPTION	POST. REF.	DEBIT	CREDIT	BALANCE

NAME ______________________ TERMS ______

DATE		DESCRIPTION	POST. REF.	DEBIT	CREDIT	BALANCE

NAME ______________________ TERMS ______

DATE		DESCRIPTION	POST. REF.	DEBIT	CREDIT	BALANCE

Name

PROBLEM 8.4A or 8.4B (continued)

Analyze:

EXTRA FORM

Name ____________________

CRITICAL THINKING PROBLEM 8.1

PURCHASES JOURNAL

PAGE ______

DATE	PURCHASED FROM	INVOICE NUMBER	INVOICE DATE	TERMS	POST. REF.	ACCOUNTS PAYABLE CREDIT	PURCHASES DEBIT	FREIGHT IN DEBIT

SALES JOURNAL

PAGE ______

	DATE	SALES SLIP NO.	CUSTOMER'S NAME	POST. REF.	ACCOUNTS RECEIVABLE DEBIT	SALES TAX PAYABLE CREDIT	SALES CREDIT	
1								1
2								2
3								3
4								4
5								5
6								6
7								7
8								8
9								9
10								10
11								11
12								12
13								13
14								14
15								15

Name

CRITICAL THINKING PROBLEM 8.1 (continued)

ACCOUNTS PAYABLE SUBSIDIARY LEDGER

NAME ________ TERMS ________

DATE		DESCRIPTION	POST. REF.	DEBIT	CREDIT	BALANCE

NAME ________ TERMS ________

DATE		DESCRIPTION	POST. REF.	DEBIT	CREDIT	BALANCE

NAME ________ TERMS ________

DATE		DESCRIPTION	POST. REF.	DEBIT	CREDIT	BALANCE

NAME ________ TERMS ________

DATE		DESCRIPTION	POST. REF.	DEBIT	CREDIT	BALANCE

NAME ________ TERMS ________

DATE		DESCRIPTION	POST. REF.	DEBIT	CREDIT	BALANCE

NAME ________ TERMS ________

DATE		DESCRIPTION	POST. REF.	DEBIT	CREDIT	BALANCE

Name

CRITICAL THINKING PROBLEM 8.1 (continued)

ACCOUNTS PAYABLE SUBSIDIARY LEDGER

NAME | TERMS

DATE		DESCRIPTION	POST. REF.	DEBIT	CREDIT	BALANCE

NAME | TERMS

DATE		DESCRIPTION	POST. REF.	DEBIT	CREDIT	BALANCE

ACCOUNTS RECEIVABLE SUBSIDIARY LEDGER

NAME | TERMS

DATE		DESCRIPTION	POST. REF.	DEBIT	CREDIT	BALANCE

NAME | TERMS

DATE		DESCRIPTION	POST. REF.	DEBIT	CREDIT	BALANCE

NAME | TERMS

DATE		DESCRIPTION	POST. REF.	DEBIT	CREDIT	BALANCE

Name

CRITICAL THINKING PROBLEM 8.1 (continued)

ACCOUNTS RECEIVABLE SUBSIDIARY LEDGER

NAME TERMS

DATE		DESCRIPTION	POST. REF.	DEBIT	CREDIT	BALANCE

NAME TERMS

DATE		DESCRIPTION	POST. REF.	DEBIT	CREDIT	BALANCE

NAME TERMS

DATE		DESCRIPTION	POST. REF.	DEBIT	CREDIT	BALANCE

NAME TERMS

DATE		DESCRIPTION	POST. REF.	DEBIT	CREDIT	BALANCE

NAME TERMS

DATE		DESCRIPTION	POST. REF.	DEBIT	CREDIT	BALANCE

NAME TERMS

DATE		DESCRIPTION	POST. REF.	DEBIT	CREDIT	BALANCE

Name ____________________

CRITICAL THINKING PROBLEM 8.1 (continued)

ACCOUNTS RECEIVABLE SUBSIDIARY LEDGER

NAME ____________________ TERMS ________

DATE		DESCRIPTION	POST. REF.	DEBIT	CREDIT	BALANCE

NAME ____________________ TERMS ________

DATE		DESCRIPTION	POST. REF.	DEBIT	CREDIT	BALANCE

GENERAL LEDGER

ACCOUNT ____________________ ACCOUNT NO. ________

DATE		DESCRIPTION	POST. REF.	DEBIT	CREDIT	BALANCE	
						DEBIT	CREDIT

ACCOUNT ____________________ ACCOUNT NO. ________

DATE		DESCRIPTION	POST. REF.	DEBIT	CREDIT	BALANCE	
						DEBIT	CREDIT

ACCOUNT ____________________ ACCOUNT NO. ________

DATE		DESCRIPTION	POST. REF.	DEBIT	CREDIT	BALANCE	
						DEBIT	CREDIT

ACCOUNT ____________________ ACCOUNT NO. ________

DATE		DESCRIPTION	POST. REF.	DEBIT	CREDIT	BALANCE	
						DEBIT	CREDIT

Name

CRITICAL THINKING PROBLEM 8.1 (continued)

GENERAL LEDGER

ACCOUNT ACCOUNT NO.

DATE		DESCRIPTION	POST. REF.	DEBIT	CREDIT	BALANCE DEBIT	BALANCE CREDIT

ACCOUNT ACCOUNT NO.

DATE		DESCRIPTION	POST. REF.	DEBIT	CREDIT	BALANCE DEBIT	BALANCE CREDIT

Name

CRITICAL THINKING PROBLEM 8.1 (continued)

Analyze:

Name

CRITICAL THINKING PROBLEM 8.2

Chapter 8 Practice Test Answer Key

Part A True-False

1. F	**11. T**
2. T	**12. F**
3. T	**13. T**
4. T	**14. F**
5. T	**15. F**
6. T	**16. T**
7. F	**17. T**
8. T	**18. F**
9. T	**19. T**
10. T	**20. F**

Part B Exercises

1. An Expense.
2. Accounts Payable Credit = Purchases Debit + Freight In Debit.
3. All Columns.
4. It is not recorded in the purchases journal at all; it is entered in the cash payments journal.
5. The Accounts Payable Column.
6. The General Journal.
7. In the Cost of Goods Sold Section.

CHAPTER 9

Cash Receipts, Cash Payments, and Banking Procedures

STUDY GUIDE

Understanding the Chapter

Objectives **1.** Record cash receipts in a cash receipts journal. **2.** Account for cash short or over. **3.** Post from the cash receipts journal to subsidiary and general ledgers. **4.** Record cash payments in a cash payments journal. **5.** Post from the cash payments journal to subsidiary and general ledgers. **6.** Demonstrate a knowledge of procedures for a petty cash fund. **7.** Demonstrate a knowledge of internal control routines for cash. **8.** Write a check, endorse checks, prepare a bank deposit slip, and maintain a checkbook balance. **9.** Reconcile the monthly bank statement. **10.** Record any adjusting entries required from the bank reconciliation. **11.** Understand how businesses use online banking to manage cash activities. **12.** Define accounting terms new to this chapter.

Reading Assignment Read Chapter 9 in the textbook. Complete the Section Self Review as you finish reading each section of the chapter, and the Comprehensive Self Review at the end of the chapter. Refer to the Chapter 9 Glossary or to the Glossary at the end of the book to find definitions for terms that are not familiar to you.

Activities

- ❑ **Thinking Critically** Answer the *Thinking Critically* questions for H&R Block and Managerial Implications
- ❑ **Discussion Questions** Answer each assigned review question in Chapter 9.
- ❑ **Exercises** Complete each assigned exercise in Chapter 9. Use the forms provided in this SGWP. The objectives covered by an exercise are given after the exercise number. If you need help with an exercise, review the portion of the chapter related to the objective(s) covered.
- ❑ **Problems A/B** Complete each assigned problem in Chapter 9. Use the forms provided in this SGWP. The objectives covered by a problem are given after the problem number. If you need help with a problem review the portion of the chapter related to the objective(s) covered.
- ❑ **Critical Thinking Problems** Complete the critical thinking problems as assigned. Use the forms provided in this SGWP.
- ❑ **Business Connections** Complete the Business Connections activities as assigned to gain a deeper understanding of Chapter 9 concepts.

Practice Tests

Complete the Practice Tests, which cover the main points in your reading assignment. Compare your answers with those in the Practice Test Answer Key for Chapter 9 at the end of this chapter. If you have answered any questions incorrectly, review the related section of the text.

Part A True-False *For each of the following statements, circle T in the answer column if the statement is true or F if the statement is false.*

T F **1.** Account numbers are recorded below the totals of each column as each summary posting from the cash payments journal is completed.

T F **2.** A cash investment by the owner in a business should be recorded in the cash receipts journal.

T F **3.** The title of a special journal makes it possible to omit much of the explanation that would be needed in a general journal entry.

T F **4.** The **Sales Tax Payable** account represents a liability of the business.

T F **5.** **Cash Short or Over** is a general ledger account that normally has a credit balance because cash tends to be short more often than over.

T F **6.** Cash received by mail should be deposited by the same person who accepts and lists it.

T F **7.** Only checks are listed on the deposit slip.

T F **8.** Checks can be identified on a deposit slip by the use of the American Bankers Association transit numbers.

T F **9.** Checks made payable to cash or to bearer need not be endorsed when deposited.

T F **10.** The money represented by deposited checks becomes available for use as soon as the deposit is made.

T F **11.** The best form of endorsement for business purposes is the restrictive endorsement, which limits the use of the check to a stated purpose.

T F **12.** Internal controls are not necessary if payments are made by check.

T F **13.** Except for petty cash payments, all payments should be made by check.

T F **14.** Correct internal control procedures require that the approval for paying all bills, writing all checks, and signing all checks should be the responsibility of the same person.

T F **15.** An adequate system of internal control over cash will provide for safeguarding both incoming and outgoing funds.

T F **16.** Each petty cash payment is entered separately in the cash payments journal.

T F **17.** The petty cash analysis sheet is a memorandum record of petty cash payments rather than a record of original entry.

T F **18.** The check to replenish the petty cash fund is written for an amount sufficient to restore the fund to its established balance.

T F **19.** When posting from the cash payments journal at the end of the month, the accountant posts the total cash payments as a single credit to cash.

T F **20.** The abbreviation "CP5" in the Posting Reference column of a ledger account indicates that the posting was made from the cash payments journal on the fifth day of the month.

T F **21.** The Other Accounts Debit column of a cash payments journal is used to record the debits that are to be posted individually.

T F **22.** Once created, login information for online bank account access should not be changed.

Part B Matching *For each numbered item, choose the matching term from the box and write the identifying letter in the answer column.*

a. NSF Check
b. Deposit in Transit
c. Outstanding checks
d. Bank reconciliation
e. Bank statement
f. Stub
g. Payee
h. Drawer
i. Deposit slip
j. Promissory note
k. Summary posting
l. Internal control
m. EFT

_______ **1.** A check on which payment has been refused because of too few funds in the issuer's account.

_______ **2.** The person or firm from whose account a check is to be paid.

_______ **3.** The form that contains all the information necessary for journalizing a transaction paid by check.

_______ **4.** The firm or person designated on the check to receive payment.

_______ **5.** The process of determining why a difference exists between the firm's accounting records and the bank records and bringing them into balance.

_______ **6.** A form on which all cash and cash items are listed before they are placed in the bank.

_______ **7.** Checks issued and recorded that have not been paid by the bank.

_______ **8.** A form received from the bank showing all transactions recorded in the depositor's account during the month.

_______ **9.** Receipts that have been deposited and entered in the firm's accounting records but have not yet been entered on the bank's records.

_______ **10.** A written promise to pay a specific amount at a specific time.

_______ **11.** A system designed to safeguard assets and to help ensure the accuracy and reliability of accounting records.

_______ **12.** The process by which a single amount is posted instead of each entry being posted separately.

_______ **13.** An electronic transfer of money from one account to another.

Demonstration Problem

On June 2, 2013, Orange Coast Legal Services received its May bank statement. Enclosed with the bank statement, shown below, was a debit memorandum for $150 for a NSF check issued by James Greene. Additionally, Check No. 177 was correctly drawn for $400 in payment of a utility bill. Orange Coast Legal Services mistakenly recorded the check as $40. The firm's checkbook contained the information shown below about deposits made and checks issued during May. The balance of the **Cash** account and the checkbook on May 31 was $37,425.

Instructions

1. Prepare a bank reconciliation statement for Orange Coast Legal Services as of May 31, 2013.
2. Record general journal entries for any items on the bank reconciliation statement that must be journalized. Date the entries May 31, 2013. Number the journal as page 17.

Checkbook information:

May 1	Balance	$40,592
1	Check 177	40
1	Check 178	800
7	Deposit	2,600
8	Check 179	900
12	Check 180	6,000
17	Check 181	720
19	Deposit	680
22	Check 182	88
23	Check 183	592
26	Deposit	1,748
29	Check 184	160
31	Deposit	925
		$37,245

First California National Bank

Orange Coast Legal Services
4312 Brea Street
Yorba Linda, CA 92885-8714

ACCOUNT NO. 77546798
PERIOD ENDING: May 31, 2013

CHECK NO.	AMOUNT	DATE	DESCRIPTION	BALANCE
			Balance last statement	40,592.00
177	400.00	6/1		40,192.00
178	800.00	6/4		39,392.00
	2,600.00	6/7	Deposit	41,992.00
179	900.00	6/8		41,092.00
180	6,000.00	6/12		35,092.00
	150.00	6/12	Debit Memorandum	34,942.00
181	720.00	6/17		34,222.00
	680.00	6/19	Deposit	34,902.00
182	88.00	6/22		34,814.00
	1,748.00	6/26	Deposit	36,562.00
	15.00	6/29	Service Charge	36,547.00

SOLUTION

Orange Coast Legal Services

Bank Reconciliation Statement

May 31, 2013

Balance on Bank Statement		36,547.00
Additions:		
Deposit of May 31 in Transit		925.00
		37,472.00
Deductions for Outstanding Checks:		
Check 183 of May 23	592.00	
Check 184 of May 29	160.00	
Total Checks Outstanding		752.00
Adjusted Bank Balance		36,720.00
Balance in Books		37,245.00
Deductions:		
NSF Check	150.00	
Recording Error, Check 177	360.00	
Bank Service Charge	15.00	525.00
Adjusted Book Balance		36,720.00

GENERAL JOURNAL PAGE 17

DATE		DESCRIPTION	POST. REF.	DEBIT	CREDIT
2013					
May	31	Accounts Receivable/James Greene		150.00	
		Cash			150.00
		To record NSF check returned by bank			
	31	Miscellaneous Expense		15.00	
		Cash			15.00
		To record bank service charge for May			

WORKING PAPERS

Name ______________________

EXERCISES 9.1, 9.2

EXERCISE 9.1

CASH RECEIPTS JOURNAL

PAGE ______

DATE	DESCRIPTION	POST. REF.	ACCOUNTS RECEIVABLE CREDIT	SALES TAX PAYABLE CREDIT	SALES CREDIT	OTHER ACCOUNTS CREDIT: ACCOUNT NAME	OTHER ACCOUNTS CREDIT: POST. REF.	OTHER ACCOUNTS CREDIT: AMOUNT	CASH DEBIT

EXERCISE 9.2

CASH PAYMENTS JOURNAL

PAGE ______

DATE	CK. NO.	DESCRIPTION	POST. REF.	ACCOUNTS PAYABLE DEBIT	OTHER ACCOUNTS DEBIT: ACCOUNT NAME	OTHER ACCOUNTS DEBIT: POST. REF.	OTHER ACCOUNTS DEBIT: AMOUNT	PURCHASES DISCOUNT CREDIT	CASH CREDIT

Name ______________________________

EXERCISES 9.3, 9.4

EXERCISE 9.3

CASH PAYMENTS JOURNAL

PAGE ____

DATE	CK. NO.	DESCRIPTION	POST. REF.	ACCOUNTS PAYABLE DEBIT	OTHER ACCOUNTS DEBIT			PURCHASES DISCOUNT CREDIT	CASH CREDIT
					ACCOUNT NAME	POST. REF.	AMOUNT		

EXERCISE 9.4

CASH PAYMENTS JOURNAL

PAGE ____

DATE	CK. NO.	DESCRIPTION	POST. REF.	ACCOUNTS PAYABLE DEBIT	OTHER ACCOUNTS DEBIT			PURCHASES DISCOUNT CREDIT	CASH CREDIT
					ACCOUNT NAME	POST. REF.	AMOUNT		

Name ____________________

EXERCISE 9.5

GENERAL JOURNAL

PAGE ______

	DATE	DESCRIPTION	POST. REF.	DEBIT	CREDIT	
1						1
2						2
3						3
4						4
5						5
6						6
7						7
8						8
9						9
10						10
11						11
12						12
13						13
14						14

Name ______________________

EXERCISE 9.6

	Bank Balance	Book Balance	Accounting Entry
1.			
2.			
3.			
4.			
5.			
6.			
7.			

EXTRA FORM

GENERAL JOURNAL PAGE ______

	DATE		DESCRIPTION	POST. REF.	DEBIT	CREDIT	
1							1
2							2
3							3
4							4
5							5
6							6
7							7
8							8
9							9
10							10
11							11
12							12
13							13
14							14

Name

EXERCISE 9.7

Name

EXERCISE 9.7 (continued)

GENERAL JOURNAL PAGE

	DATE		DESCRIPTION	POST. REF.	DEBIT	CREDIT	
1							1
2							2
3							3
4							4
5							5
6							6
7							7
8							8
9							9
10							10
11							11
12							12

Name

EXERCISE 9.8

Name

EXERCISE 9.9

GENERAL JOURNAL PAGE 21

	DATE		DESCRIPTION	POST. REF.	DEBIT	CREDIT	
1							1
2							2
3							3
4							4
5							5
6							6
7							7
8							8
9							9
10							10
11							11
12							12
13							13
14							14

Name ______________________

PROBLEM 9.1A or 9.1B

CASH RECEIPTS JOURNAL

PAGE ______

DATE	DESCRIPTION	POST. REF.	ACCOUNTS RECEIVABLE CREDIT	SALES TAX PAYABLE CREDIT	SALES CREDIT	OTHER ACCOUNTS CREDIT			CASH DEBIT
						ACCOUNT NAME	POST. REF.	AMOUNT	

Name

PROBLEM 9.1A or 9.1B (continued)

GENERAL LEDGER

ACCOUNT ______ ACCOUNT NO. ______

DATE		DESCRIPTION	POST. REF.	DEBIT	CREDIT	BALANCE DEBIT	BALANCE CREDIT

ACCOUNT ______ ACCOUNT NO. ______

DATE		DESCRIPTION	POST. REF.	DEBIT	CREDIT	BALANCE DEBIT	BALANCE CREDIT

ACCOUNT ______ ACCOUNT NO. ______

DATE		DESCRIPTION	POST. REF.	DEBIT	CREDIT	BALANCE DEBIT	BALANCE CREDIT

ACCOUNT ______ ACCOUNT NO. ______

DATE		DESCRIPTION	POST. REF.	DEBIT	CREDIT	BALANCE DEBIT	BALANCE CREDIT

ACCOUNT ______ ACCOUNT NO. ______

DATE		DESCRIPTION	POST. REF.	DEBIT	CREDIT	BALANCE DEBIT	BALANCE CREDIT

Name

PROBLEM 9.1A or 9.1B (continued)

GENERAL LEDGER

ACCOUNT ____________ ACCOUNT NO. ______

DATE	DESCRIPTION	POST. REF.	DEBIT	CREDIT	BALANCE DEBIT	BALANCE CREDIT

ACCOUNT ____________ ACCOUNT NO. ______

DATE	DESCRIPTION	POST. REF.	DEBIT	CREDIT	BALANCE DEBIT	BALANCE CREDIT

ACCOUNT ____________ ACCOUNT NO. ______

DATE	DESCRIPTION	POST. REF.	DEBIT	CREDIT	BALANCE DEBIT	BALANCE CREDIT

ACCOUNT ____________ ACCOUNT NO. ______

DATE	DESCRIPTION	POST. REF.	DEBIT	CREDIT	BALANCE DEBIT	BALANCE CREDIT

Analyze: ____________

Name ______________________________

PROBLEM 9.2A or 9.2B

CASH PAYMENTS JOURNAL

PAGE ______

DATE	CK. NO.	DESCRIPTION	POST. REF.	ACCOUNTS PAYABLE DEBIT	OTHER ACCOUNTS DEBIT			PURCHASES DISCOUNT CREDIT	CASH CREDIT
					ACCOUNT NAME	POST. REF.	AMOUNT		

Name

PROBLEM 9.2A or 9.2B (continued)

PETTY CASH ANALYSIS SHEET

PAGE

DATE	VOU. NO.	DESCRIPTION	RECEIPTS	PAYMENTS	DISTRIBUTION OF PAYMENTS				
					SUPPLIES DEBIT	DELIVERY EXPENSE DEBIT	MISC. EXPENSE DEBIT	OTHER ACCOUNTS DEBIT	
								ACCOUNT NAME	AMOUNT

Name ______________________

PROBLEM 9.2A or 9.2B (continued)

GENERAL LEDGER

ACCOUNT ______________________ ACCOUNT NO. ________

DATE	DESCRIPTION	POST. REF.	DEBIT	CREDIT	BALANCE DEBIT	BALANCE CREDIT

ACCOUNT ______________________ ACCOUNT NO. ________

DATE	DESCRIPTION	POST. REF.	DEBIT	CREDIT	BALANCE DEBIT	BALANCE CREDIT

ACCOUNT ______________________ ACCOUNT NO. ________

DATE	DESCRIPTION	POST. REF.	DEBIT	CREDIT	BALANCE DEBIT	BALANCE CREDIT

ACCOUNT ______________________ ACCOUNT NO. ________

DATE	DESCRIPTION	POST. REF.	DEBIT	CREDIT	BALANCE DEBIT	BALANCE CREDIT

ACCOUNT ______________________ ACCOUNT NO. ________

DATE	DESCRIPTION	POST. REF.	DEBIT	CREDIT	BALANCE DEBIT	BALANCE CREDIT

Name

PROBLEM 9.2A or 9.2B (continued)

GENERAL LEDGER

ACCOUNT ______ ACCOUNT NO. ______

DATE		DESCRIPTION	POST. REF.	DEBIT	CREDIT	BALANCE	
						DEBIT	CREDIT

ACCOUNT ______ ACCOUNT NO. ______

DATE		DESCRIPTION	POST. REF.	DEBIT	CREDIT	BALANCE	
						DEBIT	CREDIT

ACCOUNT ______ ACCOUNT NO. ______

DATE		DESCRIPTION	POST. REF.	DEBIT	CREDIT	BALANCE	
						DEBIT	CREDIT

ACCOUNT ______ ACCOUNT NO. ______

DATE		DESCRIPTION	POST. REF.	DEBIT	CREDIT	BALANCE	
						DEBIT	CREDIT

ACCOUNT ______ ACCOUNT NO. ______

DATE		DESCRIPTION	POST. REF.	DEBIT	CREDIT	BALANCE	
						DEBIT	CREDIT

Name

PROBLEM 9.2A or 9.2B (continued)

GENERAL LEDGER

ACCOUNT ______ ACCOUNT NO. ______

DATE		DESCRIPTION	POST. REF.	DEBIT	CREDIT	BALANCE	
						DEBIT	CREDIT

ACCOUNT ______ ACCOUNT NO. ______

DATE		DESCRIPTION	POST. REF.	DEBIT	CREDIT	BALANCE	
						DEBIT	CREDIT

ACCOUNT ______ ACCOUNT NO. ______

DATE		DESCRIPTION	POST. REF.	DEBIT	CREDIT	BALANCE	
						DEBIT	CREDIT

ACCOUNT ______ ACCOUNT NO. ______

DATE		DESCRIPTION	POST. REF.	DEBIT	CREDIT	BALANCE	
						DEBIT	CREDIT

ACCOUNT ______ ACCOUNT NO. ______

DATE		DESCRIPTION	POST. REF.	DEBIT	CREDIT	BALANCE	
						DEBIT	CREDIT

Analyze: ______

Name ______________________________

PROBLEM 9.3A or 9.3B

SALES JOURNAL

PAGE ______

	DATE	INVOICE NO.	CUSTOMER'S NAME	POST. REF.	ACCOUNTS RECEIVABLE DR./ SALES CR.	
1						1
2						2
3						3
4						4
5						5
6						6
7						7
8						8
9						9
10						10
11						11

CASH RECEIPTS JOURNAL

PAGE ______

DATE	DESCRIPTION	POST. REF.	ACCOUNTS RECEIVABLE CREDIT	SALES CREDIT	OTHER ACCOUNTS CREDIT			SALES DISCOUNTS DEBIT	CASH DEBIT
					ACCOUNT NAME	POST. REF.	AMOUNT		

Name

PROBLEM 9.3A or 9.3B (continued)

GENERAL JOURNAL PAGE

	DATE	DESCRIPTION	POST. REF.	DEBIT	CREDIT	
1						1
2						2
3						3
4						4
5						5
6						6
7						7
8						8
9						9
10						10
11						11
12						12

GENERAL LEDGER (PARTIAL)

ACCOUNT ACCOUNT NO.

DATE	DESCRIPTION	POST. REF.	DEBIT	CREDIT	BALANCE DEBIT	BALANCE CREDIT

ACCOUNT ACCOUNT NO.

DATE	DESCRIPTION	POST. REF.	DEBIT	CREDIT	BALANCE DEBIT	BALANCE CREDIT

ACCOUNT ACCOUNT NO.

DATE	DESCRIPTION	POST. REF.	DEBIT	CREDIT	BALANCE DEBIT	BALANCE CREDIT

Name

PROBLEM 9.3A or 9.3B (continued)

GENERAL LEDGER (PARTIAL)

ACCOUNT ACCOUNT NO.

DATE	DESCRIPTION	POST. REF.	DEBIT	CREDIT	BALANCE DEBIT	BALANCE CREDIT

ACCOUNT ACCOUNT NO.

DATE	DESCRIPTION	POST. REF.	DEBIT	CREDIT	BALANCE DEBIT	BALANCE CREDIT

ACCOUNT ACCOUNT NO.

DATE	DESCRIPTION	POST. REF.	DEBIT	CREDIT	BALANCE DEBIT	BALANCE CREDIT

Analyze:

Name ____________________

PROBLEM 9.4A or 9.4B

PURCHASES JOURNAL

PAGE ______

DATE	PURCHASED FROM	INVOICE NUMBER	INVOICE DATE	TERMS	POST. REF.	PURCHASES DR./ ACCOUNTS PAYABLE CR.

GENERAL JOURNAL

PAGE ______

DATE	DESCRIPTION	POST. REF.	DEBIT	CREDIT

Name

PROBLEM 9.4A or 9.4B (continued)

CASH PAYMENTS JOURNAL

PAGE

DATE	CK. NO.	DESCRIPTION	POST. REF.	ACCOUNTS PAYABLE DEBIT	OTHER ACCOUNTS DEBIT			PURCHASES DISCOUNT CREDIT	CASH CREDIT
					ACCOUNT NAME	POST. REF.	AMOUNT		

Name ____________________

PROBLEM 9.4A or 9.4B (continued)

GENERAL LEDGER

ACCOUNT ____________________ ACCOUNT NO. ______

DATE		DESCRIPTION	POST. REF.	DEBIT	CREDIT	BALANCE	
						DEBIT	CREDIT

ACCOUNT ____________________ ACCOUNT NO. ______

DATE		DESCRIPTION	POST. REF.	DEBIT	CREDIT	BALANCE	
						DEBIT	CREDIT

ACCOUNT ____________________ ACCOUNT NO. ______

DATE		DESCRIPTION	POST. REF.	DEBIT	CREDIT	BALANCE	
						DEBIT	CREDIT

ACCOUNT ____________________ ACCOUNT NO. ______

DATE		DESCRIPTION	POST. REF.	DEBIT	CREDIT	BALANCE	
						DEBIT	CREDIT

Name

PROBLEM 9.4A or 9.4B (continued)

GENERAL LEDGER

ACCOUNT ACCOUNT NO.

DATE		DESCRIPTION	POST. REF.	DEBIT	CREDIT	BALANCE DEBIT	BALANCE CREDIT

ACCOUNT ACCOUNT NO.

DATE		DESCRIPTION	POST. REF.	DEBIT	CREDIT	BALANCE DEBIT	BALANCE CREDIT

ACCOUNT ACCOUNT NO.

DATE		DESCRIPTION	POST. REF.	DEBIT	CREDIT	BALANCE DEBIT	BALANCE CREDIT

ACCOUNT ACCOUNT NO.

DATE		DESCRIPTION	POST. REF.	DEBIT	CREDIT	BALANCE DEBIT	BALANCE CREDIT

ACCOUNT ACCOUNT NO.

DATE		DESCRIPTION	POST. REF.	DEBIT	CREDIT	BALANCE DEBIT	BALANCE CREDIT

ACCOUNT ACCOUNT NO.

DATE		DESCRIPTION	POST. REF.	DEBIT	CREDIT	BALANCE DEBIT	BALANCE CREDIT

Name

PROBLEM 9.4A or 9.4B (continued)

Analyze:

EXTRA FORM

Name

PROBLEM 9.5A or 9.5B

GENERAL JOURNAL PAGE

	DATE		DESCRIPTION	POST. REF.	DEBIT	CREDIT	
1							1
2							2
3							3
4							4
5							5
6							6
7							7
8							8
9							9
10							10
11							11
12							12
13							13

Analyze:

Name

PROBLEM 9.6A or 9.6B

Name ____________

PROBLEM 9.6A or 9.6B (continued)

GENERAL JOURNAL

PAGE ______

	DATE		DESCRIPTION	POST. REF.	DEBIT	CREDIT	
1							1
2							2
3							3
4							4
5							5
6							6
7							7
8							8
9							9
10							10
11							11
12							12
13							13
14							14
15							15
16							16
17							17
18							18
19							19
20							20
21							21
22							22
23							23
24							24
25							25
26							26
27							27
28							28

Analyze: ____________

Name

PROBLEM 9.7A or 9.7B

GENERAL JOURNAL PAGE

	DATE		DESCRIPTION	POST. REF.	DEBIT	CREDIT	
1							1
2							2
3							3
4							4
5							5
6							6
7							7
8							8
9							9
10							10
11							11
12							12
13							13

Analyze:

Name ____________________

PROBLEM 9.8A or 9.8B

Name

PROBLEM 9.8A or 9.8B (continued)

GENERAL JOURNAL

PAGE

DATE	DESCRIPTION	POST. REF.	DEBIT	CREDIT

Analyze:

Name

CRITICAL THINKING PROBLEM 9.1

SALES JOURNAL

PAGE ______

DATE	SALES SLIP NO.	CUSTOMER'S NAME	POST. REF.	ACCOUNTS RECEIVABLE DEBIT	SALES TAX PAYABLE CREDIT	SALES CREDIT

PURCHASES JOURNAL

PAGE ______

DATE	PURCHASED FROM	INVOICE NUMBER	INVOICE DATE	TERMS	POST. REF.	ACCOUNTS PAYABLE CREDIT	PURCHASES DEBIT	FREIGHT IN DEBIT

Name ______________________

CRITICAL THINKING PROBLEM 9.1 (continued)

GENERAL JOURNAL PAGE ______

DATE	DESCRIPTION	POST. REF.	DEBIT	CREDIT

Name ____________________

CRITICAL THINKING PROBLEM 9.1 (continued)

CASH RECEIPTS JOURNAL

PAGE ____

DATE	DESCRIPTION	POST. REF.	ACCOUNTS RECEIVABLE CREDIT	SALES TAX PAYABLE CREDIT	SALES CREDIT	OTHER ACCOUNTS CREDIT			CASH DEBIT
						ACCOUNT NAME	POST. REF.	AMOUNT	

Name ____________________

CRITICAL THINKING PROBLEM 9.1 (continued)

CASH PAYMENTS JOURNAL

PAGE ____

DATE	CK. NO.	DESCRIPTION	POST. REF.	ACCOUNTS PAYABLE DEBIT	OTHER ACCOUNTS DEBIT			PURCHASES DISCOUNTS CREDIT	CASH CREDIT
					ACCOUNT NAME	POST. REF.	AMOUNT		

Name

CRITICAL THINKING PROBLEM 9.1 (continued)

GENERAL LEDGER

ACCOUNT ACCOUNT NO.

DATE		DESCRIPTION	POST. REF.	DEBIT	CREDIT	BALANCE	
						DEBIT	CREDIT

ACCOUNT ACCOUNT NO.

DATE		DESCRIPTION	POST. REF.	DEBIT	CREDIT	BALANCE	
						DEBIT	CREDIT

ACCOUNT ACCOUNT NO.

DATE		DESCRIPTION	POST. REF.	DEBIT	CREDIT	BALANCE	
						DEBIT	CREDIT

ACCOUNT ACCOUNT NO.

DATE		DESCRIPTION	POST. REF.	DEBIT	CREDIT	BALANCE	
						DEBIT	CREDIT

ACCOUNT ACCOUNT NO.

DATE		DESCRIPTION	POST. REF.	DEBIT	CREDIT	BALANCE	
						DEBIT	CREDIT

ACCOUNT ACCOUNT NO.

DATE		DESCRIPTION	POST. REF.	DEBIT	CREDIT	BALANCE	
						DEBIT	CREDIT

Name ____________________

CRITICAL THINKING PROBLEM 9.1 (continued)

GENERAL LEDGER

ACCOUNT ____________________ ACCOUNT NO. ________

DATE		DESCRIPTION	POST. REF.	DEBIT	CREDIT	BALANCE	
						DEBIT	CREDIT

ACCOUNT ____________________ ACCOUNT NO. ________

DATE		DESCRIPTION	POST. REF.	DEBIT	CREDIT	BALANCE	
						DEBIT	CREDIT

ACCOUNT ____________________ ACCOUNT NO. ________

DATE		DESCRIPTION	POST. REF.	DEBIT	CREDIT	BALANCE	
						DEBIT	CREDIT

ACCOUNT ____________________ ACCOUNT NO. ________

DATE		DESCRIPTION	POST. REF.	DEBIT	CREDIT	BALANCE	
						DEBIT	CREDIT

ACCOUNT ____________________ ACCOUNT NO. ________

DATE		DESCRIPTION	POST. REF.	DEBIT	CREDIT	BALANCE	
						DEBIT	CREDIT

Name

CRITICAL THINKING PROBLEM 9.1 (continued)

GENERAL LEDGER

ACCOUNT ______ ACCOUNT NO. ______

DATE		DESCRIPTION	POST. REF.	DEBIT	CREDIT	BALANCE DEBIT	BALANCE CREDIT

ACCOUNT ______ ACCOUNT NO. ______

DATE		DESCRIPTION	POST. REF.	DEBIT	CREDIT	BALANCE DEBIT	BALANCE CREDIT

ACCOUNT ______ ACCOUNT NO. ______

DATE		DESCRIPTION	POST. REF.	DEBIT	CREDIT	BALANCE DEBIT	BALANCE CREDIT

ACCOUNT ______ ACCOUNT NO. ______

DATE		DESCRIPTION	POST. REF.	DEBIT	CREDIT	BALANCE DEBIT	BALANCE CREDIT

ACCOUNT ______ ACCOUNT NO. ______

DATE		DESCRIPTION	POST. REF.	DEBIT	CREDIT	BALANCE DEBIT	BALANCE CREDIT

Name ______________________________

CRITICAL THINKING PROBLEM 9.1 (continued)

GENERAL LEDGER

ACCOUNT ______________________________ ACCOUNT NO. __________

DATE		DESCRIPTION	POST. REF.	DEBIT	CREDIT	BALANCE DEBIT	BALANCE CREDIT

ACCOUNT ______________________________ ACCOUNT NO. __________

DATE		DESCRIPTION	POST. REF.	DEBIT	CREDIT	BALANCE DEBIT	BALANCE CREDIT

ACCOUNT ______________________________ ACCOUNT NO. __________

DATE		DESCRIPTION	POST. REF.	DEBIT	CREDIT	BALANCE DEBIT	BALANCE CREDIT

ACCOUNTS RECEIVABLE SUBSIDIARY LEDGER

NAME ______________________________ TERMS __________

DATE		DESCRIPTION	POST. REF.	DEBIT	CREDIT	BALANCE

NAME ______________________________ TERMS __________

DATE		DESCRIPTION	POST. REF.	DEBIT	CREDIT	BALANCE

Name

CRITICAL THINKING PROBLEM 9.1 (continued)

ACCOUNTS RECEIVABLE SUBSIDIARY LEDGER

NAME TERMS

DATE		DESCRIPTION	POST. REF.	DEBIT	CREDIT	BALANCE

NAME TERMS

DATE		DESCRIPTION	POST. REF.	DEBIT	CREDIT	BALANCE

NAME TERMS

DATE		DESCRIPTION	POST. REF.	DEBIT	CREDIT	BALANCE

NAME TERMS

DATE		DESCRIPTION	POST. REF.	DEBIT	CREDIT	BALANCE

NAME TERMS

DATE		DESCRIPTION	POST. REF.	DEBIT	CREDIT	BALANCE

Name

CRITICAL THINKING PROBLEM 9.1 (continued)

ACCOUNTS PAYABLE SUBSIDIARY LEDGER

NAME ______________________ TERMS ________

DATE	DESCRIPTION	POST. REF.	DEBIT	CREDIT	BALANCE

NAME ______________________ TERMS ________

DATE	DESCRIPTION	POST. REF.	DEBIT	CREDIT	BALANCE

NAME ______________________ TERMS ________

DATE	DESCRIPTION	POST. REF.	DEBIT	CREDIT	BALANCE

NAME ______________________ TERMS ________

DATE	DESCRIPTION	POST. REF.	DEBIT	CREDIT	BALANCE

CRITICAL THINKING PROBLEM 9.1 (continued)

NAME ______ TERMS ______

DATE		DESCRIPTION	POST. REF.	DEBIT	CREDIT	BALANCE

NAME ______ TERMS ______

DATE		DESCRIPTION	POST. REF.	DEBIT	CREDIT	BALANCE

ACCOUNTS PAYABLE SUBSIDIARY LEDGER

NAME ______ TERMS ______

DATE		DESCRIPTION	POST. REF.	DEBIT	CREDIT	BALANCE

Analyze: ______

Name

CRITICAL THINKING PROBLEM 9.2

Name

CRITICAL THINKING PROBLEM 9.2 (continued)

Chapter 9 Practice Test Answer Key

Part A True-False

1.	T	12.	F
2.	T	13.	T
3.	T	14.	F
4.	T	15.	T
5.	F	16.	F
6.	F	17.	T
7.	F	18.	T
8.	T	19.	T
9.	F	20.	F
10.	F	21.	T
11.	T	22.	F

Part B Matching

1. a
2. h
3. f
4. g
5. d
6. i
7. c
8. e
9. b
10. j
11. l
12. k
13. m

CHAPTER 10 Payroll Computations, Records, and Payment

STUDY GUIDE

Understanding the Chapter

Objectives

1. Explain the major federal laws relating to employee earnings and withholding. **2.** Compute gross earnings of employees. **3.** Determine employee deductions for social security taxes. **4.** Determine employee deductions for Medicare taxes. **5.** Determine employee deductions for income taxes. **6.** Enter gross earnings, deductions, and net pay in the payroll register. **7.** Journalize payroll transactions in the general journal. **8.** Maintain an earnings record for each employee. **9.** Define the accounting terms new to this chapter.

Reading Assignment

Read Chapter 10 in the textbook. Complete the Section Self Review as you finish reading each section of the chapter, and the Comprehensive Self Review at the end of the chapter. Refer to the Chapter 10 Glossary or to the Glossary at the end of the book to find definitions for terms that are not familiar to you.

Activities

- ❑ **Thinking Critically** — Answer the *Thinking Critically* questions for Clif Bar and Managerial Implications.
- ❑ **Discussion Questions** — Answer each assigned review question in Chapter 10.
- ❑ **Exercises** — Complete each assigned exercise in Chapter 10. Use the forms provided in this SGWP. The objectives covered by an exercise are given after the exercise number. If you need help with an exercise, review the portion of the chapter related to the objective(s) covered.
- ❑ **Problems A/B** — Complete each assigned problem in Chapter 10. Use the forms provided in this SGWP. The objectives covered by a problem are given after the problem number. If you need help with a problem, review the portion of the chapter related to the objective(s) covered.
- ❑ **Critical Thinking Problems** — Complete the critical thinking problems as assigned. Use the forms provided in this SGWP.
- ❑ **Business Connections** — Complete the Business Connections activities as assigned to gain a deeper understanding of Chapter 10 concepts.

Practice Tests

Complete the Practice Tests, which cover the main points in your reading assignment. Compare your answers with those in the Practice Test Answer Key for Chapter 10 at the end of this chapter. If you have answered any questions incorrectly, review the related section of the text.

STUDY GUIDE

Part A True-False *For each of the following statements, circle T in the answer column if the statement is true or F if the statement is false.*

T F **1.** Payroll taxes apply to salaries and wages paid employees and to amounts paid independent contractors.

T F **2.** The Fair Labor Standards Act fixes a minimum wage for supervisory employees paid a monthly salary.

T F **3.** Employees can choose whether they want to be covered by the social security laws.

T F **4.** Most employers determine the amount of income tax to be withheld from the employee's pay by using withholding tables.

T F **5.** The Medicare tax is included in the social security tax (FICA).

T F **6.** The employee's marital status, number of exemptions, earnings for the pay period, and length of pay period are all factors in determining the amount of social security tax to be withheld.

T F **7.** The employer is required to contribute the same amount of federal unemployment tax as the amount withheld from the employee's earnings.

T F **8.** The state unemployment tax rate can be reduced by the rate charged by the federal government in the federal unemployment tax program.

T F **9.** The workers' compensation program is a federal program.

T F **10.** The payroll register provides all the information required to make a general journal entry to record the payroll.

T F **11.** An employee worked 48 hours during the week. Her regular hourly pay is $10 per hour. Her gross pay for the week is $480.00.

T F **12.** A company hires Michael Santori, CPA, to prepare monthly financial statements. Santori comes to the company's office, reviews source documents, and later returns the statements. Sestini would be classified as an employee.

Part B Matching *For each numbered item, choose the matching term from the box and write the identifying letter in the answer column.*

______ 1. A record for each employee showing the person's earnings and deductions for the period, along with cumulative data.	**a.** Employee earnings record
______ 2. Deductions to pay for medical benefits for retired persons.	**b.** Payroll register
______ 3. A tax levied on the employer to provide benefits to employees who lose their jobs.	**c.** Exempt wages
______ 4. A government publication containing withholding tables for employee taxes.	**d.** Workers' compensation insurance
______ 5. Wages before deductions.	**e.** Overtime
______ 6. Wages paid in a year above the base amount subject to a tax.	**f.** Circular E
______ 7. A columnar record that shows each employee's earnings, deductions, and net pay.	**g.** Medicare premiums
______ 8. Time worked in excess of 40 hours per week.	**h.** Unemployment tax
______ 9. Provides for funding of retirement and disability benefits.	**i.** Federal Insurance Contributions Act
______ 10. The form that employees file in order to claim the number of allowances to which they are entitled.	**j.** Employee's Withholding Allowance Certificate Form W4
	k. Gross pay

Demonstration Problem

Los Olivos Consulting Company pays its employees monthly. Payments made by the company on November 30, 2013, follow. Cumulative amounts paid to the persons named prior to November 30 are also given.

1. John Arciero, President, gross monthly salary of $17,000; gross earnings prior to November 30, $170,000.
2. Virginia Richey, Vice President, gross monthly salary of $14,000; gross earnings paid prior to November 30, $140,000.
3. Kathryn Price, independent accountant who audits the company's accounts, $17,500; gross amounts paid prior to November 30, $5,000.
4. Evelyn Wu, Treasurer, gross monthly salary of $10,060; gross earnings prior to November 30, $100,000.
5. Payment to Hankins Research Services for monthly services of Robert Hankins, a tax consultant, $7,000; amount paid to Hankins Research Services prior to November 30, $24,000.

Instructions

1. Use an earnings ceiling of $106,800, and a tax rate of 6.2 percent for social security taxes and a tax rate of 1.45 percent on all earnings for medicare taxes. Prepare a schedule showing:
   - **a.** Each employee's cumulative earnings prior to November 30.
   - **b.** Each employee's gross earnings for November.
   - **c.** The amounts to be withheld for each payroll tax from each employee's earnings; the employee's income tax withholdings are Arciero, $5,500; Richey, $3,250; Wu, $1,250.
   - **d.** The net amount due each employee.
   - **e.** The total gross earnings, the total of each payroll tax deduction, and the total net amount payable to employees.
2. Give the general journal entry to record the company's payroll on November 30. Use journal page 34. Omit description.
3. Give the general journal entry to record payments to employees on November 30.

SOLUTION

EARNINGS SCHEDULE

EMPLOYEE NAME	CUMULATIVE EARNINGS	MONTHLY PAY	SOCIAL SECURITY	MEDICARE	EMPLOYEE INCOME TAX WITHHOLDING	NET PAY
John Arciero	**$170,000.00**	**$17,000.00**	**—**	**$246.50**	**$5,500.00**	**$11,253.50**
Virginia Richey	**140,000.00**	**14,000.00**	**—**	**203.00**	**3,250.00**	**10,547.00**
Evelyn Wu	**100,000.00**	**10,000.00**	**421.60**	**145.00**	**1,250.00**	**8,183.40**
Totals	**$410,000.00**	**$41,000.00**	**$421.60**	**$594.50**	**$10,000.00**	**$29,983.90**

Kathryn Price and Robert Hankins are not employees of Los Olivos Consulting Company.

GENERAL JOURNAL PAGE **34**

	DATE		DESCRIPTION	POST. REF.	DEBIT	CREDIT	
1	**2013**						1
2	**Nov.**	**30**	**Salaries Expense**		**41 0 0 0 00**		2
3			**Social Security Tax Payable**			**4 2 1 60**	3
4			**Medicare Tax Payable**			**5 9 4 50**	4
5			**Employee Income Tax Payable**			**1 0 0 0 0 00**	5
6			**Salaries Payable**			**29 9 8 3 90**	6
7							7
8		**30**	**Salaries Payable**		**29 9 8 3 90**		8
9			**Cash**			**29 9 8 3 90**	9
10							10

WORKING PAPERS

Name ______________________

EXERCISE 10.1

EMPLOYEE NO.	HOURLY RATE	HOURS WORKED	GROSS EARNINGS

EXERCISE 10.2

HOURLY RATE	OVERTIME RATE	REGULAR HOURS WORKED	OVERTIME HOURS WORKED	REGULAR PAY	OVERTIME PAY	GROSS PAY

EXERCISE 10.3

EMPLOYEE NO.	DECEMBER SALARY	YEAR TO DATE EARNINGS THROUGH NOVEMBER 30	SOC. SEC. TAXABLE EARNINGS-DECEMBER	SOCIAL SECURITY TAX 6.20%

EXERCISE 10.4

EMPLOYEE NO.	DECEMBER SALARY	MEDICARE TAXABLE EARNINGS-DECEMBER	MEDICARE TAX 1.45%

EXERCISE 10.5

EMPLOYEE NO.	MARITAL STATUS	WITHHOLDING ALLOWANCES	WEEKLY SALARY	INCOME TAX WITHHOLDING

Name ______________________

EXERCISE 10.6

GENERAL JOURNAL PAGE ______

	DATE	DESCRIPTION	POST. REF.	DEBIT	CREDIT	
1						1
2						2
3						3
4						4
5						5
6						6
7						7
8						8
9						9
10						10
11						11
12						12
13						13
14						14
15						15

EXERCISE 10.7

GENERAL JOURNAL PAGE ______

	DATE	DESCRIPTION	POST. REF.	DEBIT	CREDIT	
1						1
2						2
3						3
4						4
5						5
6						6
7						7
8						8
9						9
10						10
11						11
12						12
13						13
14						14
15						15

Name ______________________

PROBLEM 10.1A or 10.1B

EMPLOYEE NO.	REGULAR HOURS, HOURLY RATE	HOURS WORKED	REGULAR TIME EARNINGS	OVERTIME EARNINGS	GROSS EARNINGS

Gross Pay	
Social Security Tax	
Medicare Tax	
Income Tax Withholding	
Health & Disability	
United Way	
U.S. Savings Bond	
Net Pay	

GENERAL JOURNAL

PAGE ______

	DATE		DESCRIPTION	POST. REF.	DEBIT	CREDIT	
1							1
2							2
3							3
4							4
5							5

Analyze: ______________________

Name ______________________

PROBLEM 10.2A or 10.2B

PAYROLL REGISTER WEEK BEGINNING ______ AND ENDING ______ PAID ______

NAME	NO. OF ALLOW.	MARITAL STATUS	CUMULATIVE EARNINGS	NO. OF HRS.	RATE	EARNINGS			CUMULATIVE EARNINGS	TAXABLE WAGES			DEDUCTIONS			NET AMOUNT	CHECK NO.	DISTRIBUTION
						REGULAR TIME EARNINGS	OVERTIME EARNINGS	GROSS AMOUNT		SOCIAL SECURITY	MEDICARE	FUTA	SOCIAL SECURITY	MEDICARE	INCOME TAX			WAGES EXPENSE

Name ______________________

PROBLEM 10.2A or 10.2B (continued)

GENERAL JOURNAL

PAGE ______

DATE		DESCRIPTION	POST. REF.	DEBIT	CREDIT

Analyze: ______________________

Name ____________________

PROBLEM 10.3A or 10.3B

PAYROLL REGISTER WEEK BEGINNING ____________ AND ENDING ____________ PAID ____________

NAME	NO. OF ALLOW.	MARITAL STATUS	CUMULATIVE EARNINGS	NO. OF HRS.	RATE	EARNINGS			CUMULATIVE EARNINGS
						REGULAR TIME EARNINGS	OVERTIME EARNINGS	GROSS AMOUNT	

TAXABLE WAGES		FUTA	DEDUCTIONS			NET AMOUNT	CHECK NO.	DISTRIBUTION	
SOCIAL SECURITY	MEDICARE		SOCIAL SECURITY	MEDICARE	INCOME TAX			OFFICE WAGES	DELIVERY WAGES

Name

PROBLEM 10.3A or 10.3B (continued)

GENERAL JOURNAL

PAGE

DATE		DESCRIPTION	POST. REF.	DEBIT	CREDIT

Analyze:

Name ____________________

PROBLEM 10.4A or 10.4B

EMPLOYEE NAME	CUMULATIVE EARNINGS	MONTHLY PAY	SOCIAL SECURITY	MEDICARE	EMPLOYEE INCOME TAX WITHHOLDING	NET PAY
Totals						

GENERAL JOURNAL

PAGE ____

DATE	DESCRIPTION	POST. REF.	DEBIT	CREDIT

Analyze: ____________________

Name ______________________

CRITICAL THINKING PROBLEM 10.1

EMPLOYEE NAME	CUMULATIVE EARNINGS	MONTHLY PAY	SOCIAL SECURITY	MEDICARE	EMPLOYEE INCOME TAX WITHHOLDING	NET PAY

GENERAL JOURNAL

PAGE ______

	DATE		DESCRIPTION	POST. REF.	DEBIT	CREDIT	
1							1
2							2
3							3
4							4
5							5
6							6
7							7
8							8
9							9
10							10
11							11
12							12
13							13
14							14
15							15

Analyze: ______________________

Name

CRITICAL THINKING PROBLEM 10.2

Chapter 10 Practice Test Answer Key

Part A True-False		Part B Matching	
1.	F	1.	a
2.	F	2.	g
3.	F	3.	h
4.	T	4.	f
5.	F	5.	k
6.	F	6.	c
7.	F	7.	b
8.	F	8.	e
9.	F	9.	i
10.	T	10.	j
11.	F		
12.	F		

CHAPTER 11

Payroll Taxes, Deposits, and Reports

STUDY GUIDE

Understanding the Chapter

Objectives

1. Explain how and when payroll taxes are paid to the government. **2.** Compute and record the employer's social security and Medicare taxes. **3.** Record deposit of social security, Medicare, and employee income taxes. **4.** Prepare an Employer's Quarterly Federal Tax Return, Form 941. **5.** Prepare Wage and Tax Statement (Form W-2) and Annual Transmittal of Wage and Tax Statements (Form W-3). **6.** Compute and record liability for federal and state unemployment taxes and record payment of the taxes. **7.** Prepare an Employer's Federal Unemployment Tax Return, Form 940 or 940-EZ. **8.** Compute and record workers' compensation insurance premiums. **9.** Define the accounting terms new to this chapter.

Reading Assignment

Read Chapter 11 in the textbook. Complete the textbook Section Self Review as you finish reading each section of the chapter, and Comprehensive Self Review at the end of the chapter. Refer to the Chapter 11 Glossary or to the Glossary at the end of the book to find definitions for terms that are not familiar to you.

Activities

- ❑ **Thinking Critically** — Answer the *Thinking Critically* questions for New Castle Hotels and Resorts and Managerial Implications.
- ❑ **Discussion Questions** — Answer each assigned discussion question in Chapter 11.
- ❑ **Exercises** — Complete each assigned exercise in Chapter 11. Use the forms provided in this SGWP. The objectives covered by an exercise are given after the exercise number. If you need help with an exercise, review the portion of the chapter related to the objective(s) covered.
- ❑ **Problems A/B** — Complete each assigned problem in Chapter 11. Use the forms provided in this SGWP. The objectives covered by a problem are given after the problem number. If you need help with a problem, review the portion of the chapter related to the objective(s) covered.
- ❑ **Critical Thinking Problems** — Complete the critical thinking problems as assigned. Use the forms provided in this SGWP.
- ❑ **Business Connections** — Complete the Business Connections activities as assigned to gain a deeper understanding of Chapter 11 concepts.

Practice Tests

Complete the Practice Tests, which cover the main points in your reading assignment. Compare your answers with those in the Practice Test Answer Key for Chapter 11 at the end of this chapter. If you have answered any questions incorrectly, review the related section of the text.

Part A True-False *For each of the following statements, circle T in the answer column if the statement is true or F if the statement is false.*

T F 1. Employers with a small number of employees are frequently required to deposit the entire amount of estimated workers' compensation insurance premiums early in the year.

T F 2. The credit against the federal unemployment tax is the amount actually paid to the state under its unemployment compensation insurance program.

T F 3. The premium on workers' compensation insurance is based on the federal unemployment tax.

T F 4. Premiums on workers' compensation insurance vary with the type of work performed by employees.

T F 5. The federal unemployment tax for the year is based on an audit of the payroll for the year.

T F 6. Under a typical state plan, the federal government actually receives 0.8 percent of the taxable wages because the employer is allowed credits for payments made to the state.

T F 7. The federal government grants a lower federal unemployment rate under an experience rating system to those employers who provide stable employment.

T F 8. Most states allow a credit against the FUTA for amounts paid to the federal government as SUTA.

T F 9. The employer's payroll taxes are usually recorded at the end of each payroll period, even though the cash will not be paid out until later.

T F 10. A business firm pays income tax withholding at the same rate and on the same taxable wages as employees.

T F 11. During the month immediately following the close of each calendar quarter, an employer is required to file a quarterly tax report and pay in or deposit any balance owed for social security and Medicare taxes and employees' income tax withheld.

T F 12. On each date of payment of an employee's wages, the employer must provide the employee with a statement, on Form W-2, of earnings and taxes withheld.

T F 13. Employees' individual earnings records provide much of the information needed to prepare the Employer's Quarterly Federal Tax Return, Form 941.

T F 14. Only the amount of each employee's earnings up to $7,000 each year is subject to the social security tax.

T F 15. Payments of social security tax, Medicare tax, and employee income tax withheld may be deposited, without penalty, in an authorized depository at any time up to January 31 of the following year.

T F 16. The employee must attach a Form W-3 to his or her federal income tax return.

T F 17. Each employer subject to the Federal Unemployment Compensation Tax Act must file an annual return on Form 940 by January 15 of the following year.

T F 18. Social security taxes are paid by the employer but not the employee.

Part B Matching *For each number item, choose the matching term from the box and write the identifying letter in the answer column.*

______	**1.** A tax borne equally by the employer and employee.	**a.** Workers' compensation
______	**2.** A tax paid solely by the employer.	**b.** Form 8109
______	**3.** An IRS publication containing tax rates and other information about payroll taxes.	**c.** Form 941
______	**4.** Plan providing benefits to employees who are injured or become ill on the job.	**d.** Form 940
______	**5.** A plan under which the SUTA is adjusted to reflect the unemployment experience of the employer.	**e.** Form W-3
______	**6.** A yearly form sent to the U.S. government summarizing earnings and payroll taxes withheld for the year.	**f.** Form W-2
______	**7.** A statement of earnings and deductions for each employee.	**g.** Experience rating system
______	**8.** A deposit "coupon" accompanying the employer's deposit of taxes in a commercial bank.	**h.** Publication 15, Circular E
______	**9.** An annual report to the federal government summarizing the employer's unemployment compensation tax for the year.	**i.** Federal unemployment tax
______	**10.** A quarterly report to the federal government summarizing taxable wages and payroll taxes due for the quarter.	**j.** Medicare tax

Demonstration Problem

The payroll register of the Express Printing and Copy Center showed employee earnings of $15,560 for the month ended January 31, 2013. Employee income tax withholding was $3,900. Use a social security rate of 6.2%, Medicare rate of 1.45% FUTA rate of 0.8% and SUTA rate of 5.4%. Assure all earnings are subject to these taxes.

Instructions

1. Compute the employees' social security and Medicare taxes.
2. Record the payroll for January in the general journal, page 3.
3. Compute the employer's payroll taxes for the period.
4. Prepare a general journal entry to record the employer's payroll taxes for the period.
5. Prepare a general journal entry to record the February 4 deposit of the social security, Medicare, and employee income taxes for the month.

SOLUTION

CALCULATION OF EMPLOYEE TAXES

Social security: 0.062 × $15,560	**$964.72**
Medicare: 0.0145 × $15,560	**225.62**
	$1,190.34

CALCULATION OF EMPLOYER TAXES

Social security: 0.062 × $15,560	**$964.72**
Medicare: 0.0145 × $15,560	**225.62**
FUTA: 0.008 × $15,560	**124.48**
SUTA: 0.054 × $15,560	**840.24**
	$2,155.06

SOLUTION (continued)

GENERAL JOURNAL

PAGE 3

DATE		DESCRIPTION	POST. REF.	DEBIT	CREDIT
2013					
Jan.	31	Salaries Expense		15,560.00	
		Social Security Tax Payable			964.72
		Medicare Tax Payable			225.62
		Employee Income Tax Payable			3,900.00
		Salaries Payable			10,469.66
		Payroll for January			
	31	Payroll Tax Expense		2,155.06	
		Social Security Tax Payable			964.72
		Medicare Tax Payable			225.62
		Federal Unemployment Tax Payable			124.48
		State Unemployment Tax Payable			840.24
		Payroll for January			
Feb.	4	Social Security Tax Payable		1,929.44	
		Medicare Tax Payable		451.24	
		Employee Income Tax Payable		3,900.00	
		Cash			6,280.68
		Deposit of payroll taxes withholding			

WORKING PAPERS

Name ______________________

EXERCISE 11.1

____

____

____

____

____

EXERCISE 11.2

GENERAL JOURNAL PAGE ______

	DATE	DESCRIPTION	POST. REF.	DEBIT	CREDIT	
1						1
2						2
3						3
4						4
5						5
6						6
7						7

EXERCISE 11.3

TAX	BASE	RATE	AMOUNT

EXERCISE 11.4

GENERAL JOURNAL PAGE ______

	DATE	DESCRIPTION	POST. REF.	DEBIT	CREDIT	
1						1
2						2
3						3
4						4
5						5
6						6
7						7

Name

EXERCISE 11.5

EXERCISE 11.6

GENERAL JOURNAL PAGE

	DATE		DESCRIPTION	POST. REF.	DEBIT	CREDIT	
1							1
2							2
3							3
4							4
5							5
6							6
7							7

EXERCISE 11.7

EXERCISE 11.8

WORK CLASSIFICATION	ESTIMATED EARNINGS	RATE	ESTIMATED PREMIUM

Name ____________________

PROBLEM 11.1A or 11.1B

TAX	BASE	RATE	AMOUNT

GENERAL JOURNAL PAGE 28

	DATE		DESCRIPTION	POST. REF.	DEBIT	CREDIT	
1							1
2							2
3							3
4							4
5							5
6							6
7							7
8							8
9							9
10							10
11							11
12							12

Analyze: ____________________

Name ______________________________

PROBLEM 11.2A or 11.2B

GENERAL JOURNAL

PAGE ________

DATE		DESCRIPTION	POST. REF.	DEBIT	CREDIT

Analyze: ______________________________

Name ______________________

PROBLEM 11.3A or 11.3B

GENERAL JOURNAL PAGE ______

	DATE		DESCRIPTION	POST. REF.	DEBIT	CREDIT	
1							1
2							2
3							3
4							4
5							5
6							6
7							7
8							8
9							9
10							10
11							11
12							12
13							13
14							14
15							15
16							16
17							17
18							18
19							19
20							20
21							21
22							22
23							23
24							24
25							25
26							26
27							27
28							28
29							29
30							30
31							31
32							32
33							33

Analyze: ______________________

Name

PROBLEM 11.3A or 11.3B (continued)

Form **941 for 2013: Employer's Quarterly Federal Tax Return** 9901

(Rev. January 2005) Department of the Treasury — Internal Revenue Service OMB No. 1545-0029

Employer identification number ☐☐ – ☐☐☐☐☐☐☐

Name *(not your trade name)*

Trade name *(if any)*

Address
Number Street Suite or room number
City State ZIP code

Report for this Quarter ...
(Check one.)

☐ **1:** January, February, March
☒ **2:** April, May, June
☐ **3:** July, August, September
☐ **4:** October, November, December

Read the separate instructions before you fill out this form. Please type or print within the boxes.

Part 1: Answer these questions for this quarter.

1 **Number of employees who received wages, tips, or other compensation for the pay period including:** ***Mar. 12*** **(Quarter 1),** ***June 12*** **(Quarter 2),** ***Sept. 12*** **(Quarter 3),** ***Dec. 12*** **(Quarter 4)** 1

2 **Wages, tips, and other compensation** 2

3 **Total income tax withheld from wages, tips, and other compensation** 3

4 **If no wages, tips, and other compensation are subject to social security or Medicare tax** . ☐ Check and go to line 6.

5 **Taxable social security and Medicare wages and tips:**

	Column 1		*Column 2*
5a **Taxable social security wages**	.	× .124 =	.
5b **Taxable social security tips**	.	× .124 =	.
5c **Taxable Medicare wages & tips**	.	× .029 =	.

5d **Total social security and Medicare taxes** (*Column 2,* lines 5a + 5b + 5c = line 5d) . 5d

6 **Total taxes before adjustments** (lines 3 + 5d = line 6) 6

7 **Tax adjustments** (If your answer is a negative number, write it in brackets.):

7a **Current quarter's fractions of cents** . . . .

7b **Current quarter's sick pay** . . . .

7c **Current quarter's adjustments for tips and group-term life insurance**

7d **Current year's income tax withholding** (Attach Form 941c) . .

7e **Prior quarters' social security and Medicare taxes** (Attach Form 941c)

7f **Special additions to federal income tax** (reserved use) . . . .

7g **Special additions to social security and Medicare** (reserved use)

7h **Total adjustments** (Combine all amounts: lines 7a through 7g.) 7h

8 **Total taxes after adjustments** (Combine lines 6 and 7h.) 8

9 **Advance earned income credit (EIC) payments made to employees** 9

10 **Total taxes after adjustment for advance EIC** (lines 8 – 9 = line 10) 10

11 **Total deposits for this quarter, including overpayment applied from a prior quarter** . . 11

12 **Balance due** (lines 10 – 11 = line 12) Make checks payable to the *United States Treasury* . 12

13 **Overpayment** (If line 11 is more than line 10, write the difference here.) Check one ☐ Apply to next return. ☐ Send a refund.

Next ➡

For Privacy Act and Paperwork Reduction Act Notice, see the back of the Payment Voucher. Cat. No. 17001Z Form **941**

Name

PROBLEM 11.3A or 11.3B (continued)

9902

Name *(not your trade name)*	Employer identification number

Part 2: Tell us about your deposit schedule for this quarter.

If you are unsure about whether you are a monthly schedule depositor or a semiweekly schedule depositor, see *Pub. 15 (Circular E)*, section 11.

14 ☐☐ **Write the state abbreviation for the state where you made your deposits** OR **write "MU" if you made your deposits in *multiple* states.**

15 **Check one:** ☐ **Line 10 is less than $2,500.** Go to Part 3.

☐ **You were a monthly schedule depositor for the entire quarter. Fill out your tax liability for each month.** Then go to Part 3.

Tax liability:	
Month 1	.
Month 2	.
Month 3	.
Total	. **Total must equal line 10.**

☐ **You were a semiweekly schedule depositor for any part of this quarter.** Fill out *Schedule B (Form 941): Report of Tax Liability for Semiweekly Schedule Depositors,* and attach it to this form.

Part 3: Tell us about your business. If a question does NOT apply to your business, leave it blank.

16 **If your business has closed and you do not have to file returns in the future** . . . . ☐ Check here, and

enter the final date you paid wages   /   /   .

17 **If you are a seasonal employer and you do not have to file a return for every quarter of the year** . ☐ Check here.

Part 4: May we contact your third-party designee?

Do you want to allow an employee, a paid tax preparer, or another person to discuss this return with the IRS? See the instructions for details.

☐ Yes. Designee's name

Phone (   )   –   Personal Identification Number (PIN) ☐☐☐☐☐

☐ No.

Part 5: Sign here

Under penalties of perjury, I declare that I have examined this return, including accompanying schedules and statements, and to the best of my knowledge and belief, it is true, correct, and complete.

X Sign your name here

Print name and title

Date   /   /   Phone (   )   –

Part 6: For paid preparers only *(optional)*

Preparer's signature

Firm's name

Address   EIN

ZIP code

Date   /   /   Phone (   )   –   SSN/PTIN

☐ Check if you are self-employed.

Page **2**   Form **941**

Name ______________________

PROBLEM 11.4A or 11.4B

GENERAL JOURNAL PAGE ______

	DATE		DESCRIPTION	POST. REF.	DEBIT	CREDIT	
1							1
2							2
3							3
4							4
5							5
6							6
7							7
8							8
9							9
10							10
11							11
12							12
13							13
14							14
15							15
16							16
17							17
18							18
19							19
20							20
21							21
22							22
23							23
24							24
25							25
26							26
27							27
28							28
29							29

Analyze: ______________________

Name ______________________

PROBLEM 11.5A or 11.5B

GENERAL JOURNAL PAGE ______

DATE		DESCRIPTION	POST. REF.	DEBIT	CREDIT

Analyze: ______________________

Name

PROBLEM 11.5A or 11.5B (continued)

Form **940-EZ**

Department of the Treasury
Internal Revenue Service

Employer's Annual Federal Unemployment (FUTA) Tax Return

▶ See the separate Instructions for Form 940-EZ for information on completing this form.

OMB No. 1545-1110

2013

You must complete this section. ▶

Name (as distinguished from trade name)	Calendar year
Trade name, if any	Employer identification number (EIN)
Address (number and street)	City, state, and ZIP code

T
FF
FD
FP
I
T

*Answer the questions under **Who May Use Form 940-EZ** on page 2. If you cannot use Form 940-EZ, you must use Form 940.*

A Enter the amount of contributions paid to your state unemployment fund (see the separate instructions) . . ▶ $

B (1) Enter the name of the state where you have to pay contributions . . . . ▶

(2) Enter your state reporting number as shown on your state unemployment tax return ▶

If you will not have to file returns in the future, check here (see **Who Must File** in separate instructions) **and complete and sign the return.** ▶ ☐

If this is an Amended Return, check here (see **Amended Returns** in the separate instructions) . . . . ▶ ☐

Part I Taxable Wages and FUTA Tax

1	Total payments (including payments shown on lines 2 and 3) during the calendar year for services of employees	1	
2	Exempt payments. (Explain all exempt payments, attaching additional sheets if necessary.) ▶	2	
3	Payments of more than $7,000 for services. Enter only amounts over the first $7,000 paid to each employee **(see the separate instructions)**	3	
4	Add lines 2 and 3	4	
5	**Total taxable wages** (subtract line 4 from line 1) . . . . ▶	5	
6	**FUTA tax.** Multiply the wages on line 5 by .008 and enter here. **(If the result is over $100, also complete Part II.)**	6	
7	Total FUTA tax deposited for the year, including any overpayment applied from a prior year	7	
8	**Balance due** (subtract line 7 from line 6). Pay to the "United States Treasury." . . . . ▶ If you owe more than $100, see **Depositing FUTA tax** in the separate instructions.	8	
9	**Overpayment** (subtract line 6 from line 7). Check if it is to be: ☐ **Applied to next return** or ☐ **Refunded** ▶	9	

Part II Record of Quarterly Federal Unemployment Tax Liability (Do not include state liability.) **Complete only if line 6 is over $100.**

Quarter	First (Jan. 1 – Mar. 31)	Second (Apr. 1 – June 30)	Third (July 1 – Sept. 30)	Fourth (Oct. 1 – Dec. 31)	Total for year
Liability for quarter					

Third-Party Designee

Do you want to allow another person to discuss this return with the IRS (see the separate instructions)? ☐ **Yes.** Complete the following. ☐ **No**

Designee's name ▶ Phone no. ▶ (   ) Personal identification number (PIN) ▶

Under penalties of perjury, I declare that I have examined this return, including accompanying schedules and statements, and, to the best of my knowledge and belief, it is true, correct, and complete, and that no part of any payment made to a state unemployment fund claimed as a credit was, or is to be, deducted from the payments to employees.

Signature ▶ **Title (Owner, etc.)** ▶ **Date** ▶

For Privacy Act and Paperwork Reduction Act Notice, see the separate instructions. ▼ **DETACH HERE** ▼ Cat. No. 10983G Form **940-EZ**

Form **940-V(EZ)**

Department of the Treasury
Internal Revenue Service

Payment Voucher

Use this voucher only when making a payment with your return.

OMB No. 1545-1110

2013

Complete boxes 1, 2, and 3. Do not send cash, and do not staple your payment to this voucher. Make your check or money order payable to the "United States Treasury." Be sure to enter your employer identification number (EIN), "Form 940-EZ," and "2004" on your payment.

		Dollars	Cents
1 Enter your employer identification number (EIN).	2 **Enter the amount of your payment.** ▶		
	3 Enter your business name (individual name for sole proprietors). Enter your address. Enter your city, state, and ZIP code.		

Name

PROBLEM 11.6A or 11.6B

WORK CLASSIFICATION	ESTIMATED EARNINGS	INSURANCE RATE	ESTIMATED PREMIUMS

WORK CLASSIFICATION	ACTUAL EARNINGS	INSURANCE RATE	ACTUAL PREMIUMS

Name ______________________________

PROBLEM 11.6A or 11.6B (continued)

GENERAL JOURNAL — PAGE ________

	DATE		DESCRIPTION	POST. REF.	DEBIT	CREDIT	
1							1
2							2
3							3
4							4
5							5
6							6
7							7
8							8
9							9
10							10
11							11
12							12
13							13
14							14
15							15
16							16
17							17
18							18
19							19

Analyze: ______________________________

Name

CRITICAL THINKING PROBLEM 11.1

1.

2.

3.

4.

5.

Analyze:

CRITICAL THINKING PROBLEM 11.2

1.

2. YEARLY COST—CURRENT SYSTEM

Name

CRITICAL THINKING PROBLEM 11.2 (continued)

YEARLY COST—PROPOSED SYSTEM

3.

Chapter 11 Practice Test Answer Key

Part A True-False		Part B Matching
1. T	10. F	1. j
2. F	11. T	2. i
3. F	12. F	3. h
4. T	13. T	4. a
5. F	14. F	5. g
6. T	15. F	6. e
7. F	16. F	7. f
8. F	17. F	8. b
9. T	18. F	9. d
		10. c

CHAPTER 12

Accruals, Deferrals, and the Worksheet

STUDY GUIDE

Understanding the Chapter

Objectives

1. Determine the adjustment for merchandise inventory and enter the adjustment on the worksheet. **2.** Compute adjustments for accrued and prepaid expense items and enter the adjustments on the worksheet. **3.** Compute adjustments for accrued and deferred income items and enter the adjustments on the worksheet. **4.** Complete a ten-column worksheet. **5.** Define the accounting terms new to this chapter.

Reading Assignment

Read Chapter 12 in the textbook. Complete the textbook Section Self Review as you finish reading each section of the chapter, and the Comprehensive Self Review at the end of the chapter. Refer to the Chapter 12 Glossary or to the Glossary at the end of the book to find definitions for terms that are not familiar to you.

Activities

- ❑ **Thinking Critically** — Answer the *Thinking Critically* questions for Urban Outfitters and Managerial Implications.
- ❑ **Discussion Questions** — Answer each assigned discussion question in Chapter 12.
- ❑ **Exercises** — Complete each assigned exercise in Chapter 12. Use the forms provided in this SGWP. The objectives covered by an exercise are given after the exercise number. If you need help with an exercise, review the portion of the chapter related to the objective(s) covered.
- ❑ **Problems A/B** — Complete each assigned problem in Chapter 12. Use the forms provided in this SGWP. The objectives covered by a problem are given after the problem number. If you need help with a problem, review the portion of the chapter related to the objective(s) covered.
- ❑ **Critical Thinking Problems** — Complete the critical thinking problems as assigned. Use the forms provided in this SGWP.
- ❑ **Business Connections** — Complete the Business Connections activities as assigned to gain a deeper understanding of Chapter 12 concepts.

Practice Tests

Complete the Practice Tests, which cover the main points in your reading assignment. Compare your answers with those in the Practice Test Answer Key for Chapter 12 at the end of this chapter. If you have answered any questions incorrectly, review the related section of the text.

STUDY GUIDE

Part A True-False *For each of the following statements, circle T in the answer column if the statement is true or F if the statement is false.*

T F 1. After the amounts shown in the Adjusted Trial Balance section have been extended, the difference between the total debits and total credits in the balance sheet section represents the net income or loss for the period.

T F 2. The Adjusted Trial Balance column of the worksheet tests only the arithmetic accuracy of the worksheet to that point in the worksheet and statement preparation process.

T F 3. The accountant completes the worksheet and prepares the financial statements as soon as all adjustments have been entered on the worksheet.

T F 4. The net income for the business is entered as a debit entry in the Balance Sheet section and as a credit entry in the Income Statement section of the worksheet.

T F 5. Office or store supplies that have been paid for in cash do not need any adjusting entries.

T F 6. An adjustment for depreciation results in an entry debiting the **Depreciation Expense** account and crediting the **Equipment** account.

T F 7. On the trial balance, the **Store Supplies** account shows a debit balance of $300. A physical count showed supplies on hand of $80. The adjusting entry includes a debit of $80 to the **Store Supplies Expense** account.

T F 8. At the end of an accounting period, an adjustment is needed to record as an expense any part of the balance in an asset account that has been used up or has expired.

T F 9. The unadjusted trial balance figures for accumulated depreciation accounts do not include depreciation for the current period.

T F 10. The **Unearned Subscriptions Income** account will appear in the Liabilities section of the balance sheet.

T F 11. In the "adjustments" column of the worksheet, the **Merchandise Inventory** is debited for the amount of ending inventory and credited for the amount of beginning inventory.

T F 12. Under the accrual basis of accounting, purchases are recorded after the purchase has been paid.

T F 13. The **Interest Expense** account must be adjusted if an interest-bearing note payable is outstanding at the end of the fiscal period and interest has not been paid on that date.

T F 14. In most cases, **Prepaid Interest Expense** will be classified in the Assets section on the balance sheet.

T F 15. **Interest Receivable** is usually classified as a revenue account.

T F 16. The entry to record accrued interest on notes payable is a debit to **Interest Expense** and a credit to **Interest Receivable.**

T F 17. Deferred income has been earned but not recorded, while accrued income has been recorded but not earned.

T F 18. Adjusting entries are recorded in the general journal after the worksheet and the financial statements are completed.

T F 19. The beginning merchandise inventory does not appear in the Adjusted Trial Balance.

T F 20. The **Drawing** account balance is extended to the Debit column in the Income Statement section.

T F 21. The statement of owner's equity should be prepared after the income statement is prepared.

T F 22. The financial statements are prepared directly from the worksheet.

T F 23. In preparing financial statements, it is unnecessary to make adjustments for relatively small items because they are immaterial and will not affect the statements.

T F 24. A prepaid expense incorrectly charged to expense in an accounting period results in an understatement of net income in that period and an overstatement of net income in the following period.

T F 25. The accounts should be adjusted when preparing monthly or quarterly statements.

Part B Exercise *In each of the following independent cases give the general journal entry to adjust the accounts for the year on December 31, 2013. Omit the descriptions.*

1. Store supplies costing $1,600 were purchased during the year and were charged to the **Store Supplies** account. At the end of the year, supplies costing $400 were on hand.

GENERAL JOURNAL PAGE ______

	DATE	DESCRIPTION	POST. REF.	DEBIT	CREDIT	
1						1
2						2

2. On December 1, 2013 the company gave a $4,000 note payable to a supplier. The note bears interest at 6 percent.

GENERAL JOURNAL PAGE ______

	DATE	DESCRIPTION	POST. REF.	DEBIT	CREDIT	
1						1
2						2

3. On October 1, 2013, the company received a four-month, 8 percent note for $3,500 from settlement of an overdue account. No interest has been recorded on the note.

GENERAL JOURNAL PAGE ______

	DATE	DESCRIPTION	POST. REF.	DEBIT	CREDIT	
1						1
2						2

4. On November 1, 2013, the company purchased a one-year insurance policy for $2,400. The amount was charged to **Prepaid Insurance.**

GENERAL JOURNAL PAGE ______

	DATE	DESCRIPTION	POST. REF.	DEBIT	CREDIT	
1						1
2						2

5. During 2013, the Irvine Quakes minor league hockey team received $900,000 from the sale of season tickets for 20 home games. The Unearned Season Tickets Income account was credited upon receipt of the cash. As of December 31, 8 home games had been played.

GENERAL JOURNAL PAGE ______

	DATE	DESCRIPTION	POST. REF.	DEBIT	CREDIT	
1						1
2						2

Demonstration Problem

The trial balance for Pietro's Imports on December 31, 2013, the end of its accounting period, is shown on the worksheet.

Instructions

1. Complete the worksheet for the year, using the following information:
   - **a-b.** Ending merchandise inventory, $108,570.
   - **c.** Uncollectible accounts expense, $1,900.
   - **d.** Supplies on hand December 31, $680.
   - **e.** Depreciation on store equipment, $8,100.
   - **f.** Depreciation on office equipment, $3,050.
   - **g.** Accrued sales salaries, $4,000; accrued office salaries, $750.
   - **h.** Tax on accrued salaries: social security, $294.50; Medicare, $68.88.
2. Journalize the adjusting entries on page 16 of the general journal.

SOLUTION

Pietro's Imports

Worksheet

December 31, 2013

	ACCOUNT NAME	TRIAL BALANCE DEBIT	TRIAL BALANCE CREDIT	ADJUSTMENTS DEBIT	ADJUSTMENTS CREDIT
1	**Cash**	39,810.00			
2	**Accounts Receivable**	32,340.00			
3	**Allowance for Doubtful Accounts**		506.00		(c) 1,900.00
4	**Merchandise Inventory**	116,780.00		(b)108,570.00	(a)116,780.00
5	**Supplies**	10,600.00			(d) 9,920.00
6	**Store Equipment**	84,000.00			
7	**Accumulated Depreciation—Store Equip.**		16,590.00		(e) 8,100.00
8	**Office Equipment**	25,700.00			
9	**Accumulated Depreciation—Office Equip.**		7,033.00		(f) 3,050.00
10	**Accounts Payable**		22,560.00		
11	**Salaries Payable**				(g) 4,750.00
12	**Social Security Tax Payable**				(h) 294.50
13	**Medicare Tax Payable**				(h) 68.88
14	**Pietro Canzone, Capital**		230,764.00		
15	**Pietro Canzone, Drawing**	26,000.00			
16	**Income Summary**			(a)116,780.00	(b)108,570.00
17	**Sales**		424,642.00		
18	**Sales Returns and Allowances**	8,155.00			
19	**Purchases**	197,534.00			
20	**Purchase Returns and Allowances**		1,200.00		
21	**Purchase Discounts**		600.00		
22	**Freight In**	12,260.00			
23	**Sales Salaries Expense**	94,580.00		(g) 4,000.00	
24	**Rent Expense**	31,000.00			
25	**Advertising Expense**	12,045.00			
26	**Supplies Expense**			(d) 9,920.00	
27	**Depreciation Expense—Store Equipment**			(e) 8,100.00	
28	**Office Salaries Expense**	17,645.00		(g) 750.00	
29	**Payroll Taxes Expense**			(h) 363.38	
30	**Depreciation Expense—Office Equipment**			(f) 3,050.00	
31	**Uncollectible Accounts Expense**			(c) 1,900.00	
32		708,449.00	708,449.00	253,433.38	253,433.38
33	**Net Income**				
34					
35					

SOLUTION (continued)

Adjusted Trial Balance Debit	Adjusted Trial Balance Credit	Income Statement Debit	Income Statement Credit	Balance Sheet Debit	Balance Sheet Credit
39,810.00				39,810.00	
32,340.00				32,340.00	
	6,960.00				6,960.00
108,570.00				108,570.00	
680.00				680.00	
84,000.00				84,000.00	
	24,690.00				24,690.00
25,700.00				25,700.00	
	10,083.00				10,083.00
	22,560.00				22,560.00
	4,750.00				4,750.00
	294.50				294.50
	68.88				68.88
	230,764.00				230,764.00
26,000.00				26,000.00	
116,780.00	108,570.00	116,780.00	108,570.00		
	424,642.00		424,642.00		
8,155.00		8,155.00			
197,534.00		197,534.00			
	1,200.00		1,200.00		
	600.00		600.00		
12,260.00		12,260.00			
98,580.00		98,580.00			
31,000.00		31,000.00			
12,045.00		12,045.00			
9,920.00		9,920.00			
8,100.00		8,100.00			
18,395.00		18,395.00			
363.38		363.38			
3,050.00		3,050.00			
1,900.00		1,900.00			
835,182.38	835,182.38	518,082.38	535,012.00	317,100.00	300,170.38
		16,929.62			16,929.62
		535,012.00	535,012.00	317,100.00	317,100.00

SOLUTION (continued)

GENERAL JOURNAL

PAGE 16

DATE		DESCRIPTION	POST. REF.	DEBIT	CREDIT
2013					
		(a)			
Dec.	31	Income Summary		116,780.00	
		Merchandise Inventory			116,780.00
		Close beginning merchandise inventory			
		(b)			
	31	Merchandise Inventory		108,570.00	
		Income Summary			108,570.00
		Record ending merchandise inventory			
		(c)			
	31	Uncollectible Accounts Expense		1,900.00	
		Allowance for Doubtful Accounts			1,900.00
		Record estimated uncollectible accounts expense			
		(d)			
	31	Supplies Expense		9,920.00	
		Supplies			9,920.00
		Record supplies used during year			
		(e)			
	31	Depreciation Expense—Store Equipment		8,100.00	
		Accumulated Depreciation—Store Equipment			8,100.00
		Record depreciation on store equipment for year			
		(f)			
	31	Depreciation Expense—Office Equipment		3,050.00	
		Accumulated Depreciation—Office Equipment			3,050.00
		Record depreciation on office equipment for year			
		(g)			
	31	Sales Salaries Expense		4,000.00	
		Office Salaries Expense		750.00	
		Salaries Payable			4,750.00
		Record accrued salaries			
		(h)			
	31	Payroll Taxes Expense		363.38	
		Social Security Tax Payable			294.50
		Medicare Tax Payable			68.88
		Record accrued payroll taxes			

WORKING PAPERS

Name ______________________

EXERCISE 12.1

GENERAL JOURNAL

PAGE ______

	DATE		DESCRIPTION	POST. REF.	DEBIT	CREDIT	
1							1
2							2
3							3
4							4
5							5
6							6
7							7

EXERCISE 12.2

____

____

____

EXERCISE 12.3

GENERAL JOURNAL

PAGE ______

	DATE		DESCRIPTION	POST. REF.	DEBIT	CREDIT	
1							1
2							2
3							3
4							4
5							5
6							6
7							7
8							8
9							9
10							10
11							11
12							12
13							13
14							14
15							15
16							16
17							17
18							18

Name ______________________

EXERCISE 12.4

GENERAL JOURNAL

PAGE ______

	DATE	DESCRIPTION	POST. REF.	DEBIT	CREDIT	
1						1
2						2
3						3
4						4
5						5
6						6
7						7
8						8
9						9
10						10
11						11
12						12
13						13

EXERCISE 12.5

GENERAL JOURNAL

PAGE ______

	DATE	DESCRIPTION	POST. REF.	DEBIT	CREDIT	
1						1
2						2
3						3
4						4
5						5
6						6
7						7
8						8

EXERCISE 12.6

GENERAL JOURNAL

PAGE ______

	DATE	DESCRIPTION	POST. REF.	DEBIT	CREDIT	
1						1
2						2
3						3
4						4

Name

EXERCISE 12.7

GENERAL JOURNAL

PAGE

	DATE		DESCRIPTION	POST. REF.	DEBIT	CREDIT	
1							1
2							2
3							3
4							4
5							5
6							6
7							7
8							8
9							9
10							10
11							11
12							12
13							13

Name

PROBLEM 12.1A or 12.1B

GENERAL JOURNAL

PAGE

DATE		DESCRIPTION	POST. REF.	DEBIT	CREDIT

Name ______________________

PROBLEM 12.1A or 12.1B (continued)

GENERAL JOURNAL PAGE ______

DATE	DESCRIPTION	POST. REF.	DEBIT	CREDIT

Analyze: ______________________

Name

PROBLEM 12.2A or 12.2B

GENERAL JOURNAL PAGE 1

DATE		DESCRIPTION	POST. REF.	DEBIT	CREDIT

Name ______________________

PROBLEM 12.2A or 12.2B (continued)

GENERAL JOURNAL PAGE 2

DATE		DESCRIPTION	POST. REF.	DEBIT	CREDIT

Analyze: ______________________

Name

PROBLEM 12.3A or 12.3B

	ACCOUNT NAME	TRIAL BALANCE		ADJUSTMENTS	
		DEBIT	CREDIT	DEBIT	CREDIT
1					
2					
3					
4					
5					
6					
7					
8					
9					
10					
11					
12					
13					
14					
15					
16					
17					
18					
19					
20					
21					
22					
23					
24					
25					
26					
27					
28					
29					
30					
31					
32					

Name ______________________

PROBLEM 12.3A or 12.3B (continued)

ADJUSTED TRIAL BALANCE		INCOME STATEMENT		BALANCE SHEET		
DEBIT	CREDIT	DEBIT	CREDIT	DEBIT	CREDIT	
						1
						2
						3
						4
						5
						6
						7
						8
						9
						10
						11
						12
						13
						14
						15
						16
						17
						18
						19
						20
						21
						22
						23
						24
						25
						26
						27
						28
						29
						30
						31
						32

Analyze: ______________________

Name ______________________

PROBLEM 12.4A or 12.4B

	ACCOUNT NAME	TRIAL BALANCE		ADJUSTMENTS	
		DEBIT	CREDIT	DEBIT	CREDIT
1					
2					
3					
4					
5					
6					
7					
8					
9					
10					
11					
12					
13					
14					
15					
16					
17					
18					
19					
20					
21					
22					
23					
24					
25					
26					
27					
28					
29					
30					
31					
32					
33					
34					

Name ____________________

PROBLEM 12.4A or 12.4B (continued)

ADJUSTED TRIAL BALANCE		INCOME STATEMENT		BALANCE SHEET		
DEBIT	CREDIT	DEBIT	CREDIT	DEBIT	CREDIT	
						1
						2
						3
						4
						5
						6
						7
						8
						9
						10
						11
						12
						13
						14
						15
						16
						17
						18
						19
						20
						21
						22
						23
						24
						25
						26
						27
						28
						29
						30
						31
						32
						33
						34

Name

PROBLEM 12.4A or 12.4B (continued)

	ACCOUNT NAME	TRIAL BALANCE DEBIT	TRIAL BALANCE CREDIT	ADJUSTMENTS DEBIT	ADJUSTMENTS CREDIT
1					
2					
3					
4					
5					
6					
7					
8					
9					
10					
11					
12					
13					
14					
15					
16					
17					
18					
19					
20					
21					
22					
23					
24					
25					
26					
27					
28					
29					
30					
31					
32					

Name ______________________

PROBLEM 12.4A or 12.4B (continued)

ADJUSTED TRIAL BALANCE		INCOME STATEMENT		BALANCE SHEET	
DEBIT	CREDIT	DEBIT	CREDIT	DEBIT	CREDIT

Analyze: ______________________

Name ______________________

PROBLEM 12.5A or 12.5B

	ACCOUNT NAME	TRIAL BALANCE		ADJUSTMENTS	
		DEBIT	CREDIT	DEBIT	CREDIT
1					
2					
3					
4					
5					
6					
7					
8					
9					
10					
11					
12					
13					
14					
15					
16					
17					
18					
19					
20					
21					
22					
23					
24					
25					
26					
27					
28					
29					
30					
31					
32					
33					
34					

Name ______________________________

PROBLEM 12.5A or 12.5B (continued)

ADJUSTED TRIAL BALANCE		INCOME STATEMENT		BALANCE SHEET		
DEBIT	CREDIT	DEBIT	CREDIT	DEBIT	CREDIT	
						1
						2
						3
						4
						5
						6
						7
						8
						9
						10
						11
						12
						13
						14
						15
						16
						17
						18
						19
						20
						21
						22
						23
						24
						25
						26
						27
						28
						29
						30
						31
						32
						33
						34

Name

PROBLEM 12.5A or 12.5B (continued)

	ACCOUNT NAME	TRIAL BALANCE		ADJUSTMENTS	
		DEBIT	CREDIT	DEBIT	CREDIT
1					
2					
3					
4					
5					
6					
7					
8					
9					
10					
11					
12					
13					
14					
15					
16					
17					
18					
19					
20					
21					
22					
23					
24					
25					
26					
27					
28					
29					
30					
31					
32					

Name

PROBLEM 12.5A or 12.5B (continued)

ADJUSTED TRIAL BALANCE		INCOME STATEMENT		BALANCE SHEET		
DEBIT	CREDIT	DEBIT	CREDIT	DEBIT	CREDIT	
						1
						2
						3
						4
						5
						6
						7
						8
						9
						10
						11
						12
						13
						14
						15
						16
						17
						18
						19
						20
						21
						22
						23
						24
						25
						26
						27
						28
						29
						30
						31
						32

Analyze:

Name ____________________

PROBLEM 12.6A or 12.6B

ACCOUNT NAME	TRIAL BALANCE		ADJUSTMENTS	
	DEBIT	CREDIT	DEBIT	CREDIT

Name

PROBLEM 12.6A or 12.6B (continued)

ADJUSTED TRIAL BALANCE		INCOME STATEMENT		BALANCE SHEET		
DEBIT	CREDIT	DEBIT	CREDIT	DEBIT	CREDIT	
						1
						2
						3
						4
						5
						6
						7
						8
						9
						10
						11
						12
						13
						14
						15
						16
						17
						18
						19
						20
						21
						22
						23
						24
						25
						26
						27
						28
						29
						30
						31
						32
						33
						34
						35

Name ______________________

CRITICAL THINKING PROBLEM 12.1

	ACCOUNT NAME	TRIAL BALANCE		ADJUSTMENTS	
		DEBIT	CREDIT	DEBIT	CREDIT
1					
2					
3					
4					
5					
6					
7					
8					
9					
10					
11					
12					
13					
14					
15					
16					
17					
18					
19					
20					
21					
22					
23					
24					
25					
26					
27					
28					
29					
30					
31					
32					
33					

Name

CRITICAL THINKING PROBLEM 12.1 (continued)

ADJUSTED TRIAL BALANCE		INCOME STATEMENT		BALANCE SHEET		
DEBIT	CREDIT	DEBIT	CREDIT	DEBIT	CREDIT	
						1
						2
						3
						4
						5
						6
						7
						8
						9
						10
						11
						12
						13
						14
						15
						16
						17
						18
						19
						20
						21
						22
						23
						24
						25
						26
						27
						28
						29
						30
						31
						32
						33

Name ______________________

CRITICAL THINKING PROBLEM 12.1 (continued)

	ACCOUNT NAME	TRIAL BALANCE		ADJUSTMENTS	
		DEBIT	CREDIT	DEBIT	CREDIT
1					
2					
3					
4					
5					
6					
7					
8					
9					
10					
11					
12					
13					
14					
15					
16					
17					
18					
19					
20					
21					
22					
23					
24					
25					
26					
27					
28					
29					
30					
31					
32					

CRITICAL THINKING PROBLEM 12.1 (continued)

	ADJUSTED TRIAL BALANCE		INCOME STATEMENT		BALANCE SHEET		
	DEBIT	CREDIT	DEBIT	CREDIT	DEBIT	CREDIT	
							1
							2
							3
							4
							5
							6
							7
							8
							9
							10
							11
							12
							13
							14
							15
							16
							17
							18
							19
							20
							21
							22
							23
							24
							25
							26
							27
							28
							29
							30
							31
							32

Name ____________________

CRITICAL THINKING PROBLEM 12.1 (continued)

GENERAL JOURNAL PAGE 30

DATE	DESCRIPTION	POST. REF.	DEBIT	CREDIT

Name

CRITICAL THINKING PROBLEM 12.1 (continued)

GENERAL JOURNAL

PAGE 32

DATE		DESCRIPTION	POST. REF.	DEBIT	CREDIT

Name

CRITICAL THINKING PROBLEM 12.1 (continued)

a. Net Sales

b. Net Delivered Cost of Purchases

c. Cost of Goods Sold

d. Net Income (from worksheet)

e. Capital, December 31

Analyze:

Name

CRITICAL THINKING PROBLEM 12.2

1.

2.

Name ____________________

Chapter 12 Practice Test Answer Key

Part A True-False

1. T
2. T
3. T
4. F
5. F
6. F
7. F
8. T
9. T
10. T
11. T
12. F
13. T
14. T
15. F
16. F
17. F
18. T
19. T
20. F
21. T
22. T
23. F
24. T
25. T

Part B Exercises

GENERAL JOURNAL

PAGE______

DATE		DESCRIPTION	POST. REF.	DEBIT	CREDIT
		Adjusting Entries			
2013		(Adjustment 1)			
Dec.	31	Supplies Expense		1,200.00	
		Store Supplies			1,200.00
		(Adjustment 2)			
	31	Interest Expense		20.00	
		Interest Payable			20.00
		(Adjustment 3)			
	31	Interest Receivable		70.00	
		Interest Income			70.00
		(Adjustment 4)			
	31	Insurance Expense		400.00	
		Prepaid Insurance			400.00
		(Adjustment 5)			
	31	Unearned Season Tickets Income		360,000.00	
		Season Tickets Income			360,000.00

CHAPTER 13

Financial Statements and Closing Procedures

STUDY GUIDE

Understanding the Chapter

Objectives 1. Prepare a classified income statement from the worksheet. 2. Prepare a statement of owner's equity from the worksheet. 3. Prepare a classified balance sheet from the worksheet. 4. Journalize and post the adjusting entries. 5. Journalize and post the closing entries. 6. Prepare a postclosing trial balance. 7. Journalize and post reversing entries. 8. Define the accounting terms new to this chapter.

Reading Assignment Read Chapter 13 in the textbook. Complete the textbook Section Self Review as you finish reading each section of the chapter, and the Comprehensive Self Review at the end of the chapter. Refer to the Chapter 13 Glossary or to the Glossary at the end of the book to find definitions for terms that are not familiar to you.

Activities

- ❑ **Thinking Critically** Answer the *Thinking Critically* questions for Whole Foods Market and Managerial Implications.
- ❑ **Discussion Questions** Answer each assigned discussion question in Chapter 13.
- ❑ **Exercises** Complete each assigned exercise in Chapter 13. Use the forms provided in this SGWP. The objectives covered by an exercise are given after the exercise number. If you need help with an exercise, review the portion of the chapter related to the objective(s) covered.
- ❑ **Problems A/B** Complete each assigned problem in Chapter 13. Use the forms provided in this SGWP. The objectives covered by a problem are given after the problem number. If you need help with a problem review the portion of the chapter related to the objective(s) covered.
- ❑ **Critical Thinking Problems** Complete the critical thinking problems as assigned. Use the forms provided in this SGWP.
- ❑ **Business Connections** Complete the Business Connections activities as assigned to gain a deeper understanding of Chapter 13 concepts.

Practice Tests

Complete the Practice Tests, which cover the main points in your reading assignment. Compare your answers with those in the Practice Test Answer Key for Chapter 13 at the end of this chapter. If you have answered any questions incorrectly, review the related section of text.

Part A True-False *True-False For each of the following statements, circle T in the answer column if the statement is true or F if the statement is false.*

T F **1.** A company reported net sales of $1,000,000 and cost of goods sold of $600,000. The gross profit percentage is 60%.

T F **2.** Some accounts adjusted in the Adjustment columns of the worksheet do not require a reversing entry.

T F **3.** **Interest Payable** and **Depreciation Expense** are typical of accounts that do not require reversing entries.

T F **4.** Cash, accounts receivable, merchandise inventory, and equipment are classified as current assets.

T F **5.** Reversing entries are not required, but are highly recommended in order to improve efficiency and reduce errors.

T F **6.** In closing the **Income Summary** account, the net income or loss is closed into the owner's capital account.

T F **7.** Closing journal entries for December 31, 2013 should be reversed on January 1, 2014.

T F **8.** **Income Summary** is credited for the total of the expenses and the beginning inventory.

T F **9.** The ending merchandise inventory is recorded in the accounting records by an adjusting entry.

T F **10.** Adjustments are posted from the worksheet to the general ledger accounts.

T F **11.** The depreciation expense for the store equipment appears in the Plant and Equipment section of the classified balance sheet.

T F **12.** The net income or loss from operations shown on the classified income statement is the difference between gross profit on sales and total operating expenses.

T F **13.** The Cost of Goods Sold section of the classified income statement includes information about the beginning and ending merchandise inventory and the purchases and net sales made during the year.

T F **14.** Current liabilities are debts that are due for payment after one year from the balance sheet date.

T F **15.** The gross profit on sales shown on the classified income statement is the difference between the net sales and the operating expenses.

T F **16.** Short-term notes receivable, cash, accounts receivable, merchandise inventory and prepaid expense items appear in the Current Assets section of the classified balance sheet.

T F **17.** The postclosing trial balance shows essentially the same account balances that appear in the balance sheet.

T F **18.** It is desirable to prepare a postclosing trial balance after the adjusting and closing entries have been journalized and posted.

T F **19.** The **Income Summary** account is closed at the end of the period.

T F 20. Asset, liability, and owner's capital accounts are the only accounts carried forward from one year to the next.

T F 21. The information needed to close the revenue and expense accounts is taken directly from the ledger accounts to ensure accuracy.

T F 22. The revenue and expense accounts are the only accounts carried forward from one year to the next.

T F 23. After all adjustments have been journalized and posted, the ledger account balances should be the same as the post-closing trial balance amounts.

T F 24. After completing the worksheet and the financial statements, adjustments are entered in the general journal.

T F 25. The drawing account is closed into the **Income Summary** account as one of the last closing entries.

Demonstration Problem

A partial worksheet showing the end-of-year operating results for Sports Warehouse for 2013 follows.

Instructions

1. Prepare a classified income statement. Sports Warehouse does not classify its operating expenses as selling and administrative expenses.
2. Prepare a statement of owner's equity. No additional investments were made during the period.
3. Prepare a classified balance sheet as of December 31, 2013. All notes payable are due within one year.
4. Journalize the closing entries on page 45 of the general journal.
5. Compute the gross profit percentage for the year ended December 31, 2013. Round your answer to one decimal.
6. Compute the current ratio at December 31, 2013. Round your answer to two decimal places.
7. Compute the inventory turnover ratio for the year ended December 31, 2013. Round your answer to two decimal places.

DEMONSTRATION PROBLEM (continued)

Sports Warehouse
Worksheet (Partial)
Year Ended December 31, 2013

	ACCOUNT NAME	INCOME STATEMENT		BALANCE SHEET	
		DEBIT	CREDIT	DEBIT	CREDIT
1	Cash			24,285.00	
2	Accounts Receivable			61,258.00	
3	Allowance for Doubtful Accounts				5,930.00
4	Merchandise Inventory			197,214.00	
5	Supplies			3,512.00	
6	Prepaid Insurance			37,000.00	
7	Equipment			83,290.00	
8	Accumulated Depreciation—Equipment				24,330.00
9	Notes Payable				47,500.00
10	Accounts Payable				44,860.00
11	Social Security Tax Payable				2,683.00
12	Medicare Tax Payable				845.00
13	Salaries Payable				7,530.00
14	Interest Payable				3,660.00
15	Raul Flores, Capital				260,730.00
16	Raul Flores, Drawing			50,000.00	
17	Income Summary	201,345.00	197,214.00		
18	Sales		625,690.00		
19	Sales Returns and Allowances	11,950.00			
20	Purchases	280,174.00			
21	Purchases Returns and Allowances		10,440.00		
22	Freight In	11,410.00			
23	Purchases Discounts		11,921.00		
24	Telephone Expense	4,171.00			
25	Salaries Expense	241,380.00			
26	Payroll Tax Expense	13,104.00			
27	Supplies Expense	6,060.00			
28	Insurance Expense	5,000.00			
29	Depreciation Expense—Equipment	7,420.00			
30	Uncollectible Accounts Expense	2,600.00			
31	Interest Expense	2,160.00			
32	Totals	786,774.00	845,265.00	456,559.00	398,068.00
33	Net Income	58,491.00			58,491.00
34		845,265.00	845,265.00	456,559.00	456,559.00
35					

SOLUTION

(1.)

Sports Warehouse
Income Statement
Year Ended December 31, 2013

Operating Revenue				
Sales				625 690 00
Less Sales Returns and Allowances				11 950 00
Net Sales				613 740 00
Cost of Goods Sold				
Merchandise Inventory, Jan. 1, 2013			201 345 00	
Purchases		280 174 00		
Freight In		11 410 00		
Delivered Cost of Purchases		291 584 00		
Less Purchase Returns and Allow.	10 440 00			
Purchase Discounts	11 921 00	22 361 00		
Net Delivered Cost of Purchases			269 223 00	
Total Merchandise Available for Sale			470 568 00	
Less Merchandise Inv., Dec. 31, 2013			197 214 00	
Cost of Goods Sold				273 354 00
Gross Profit on Sales				340 386 00
Operating Expenses				
Telephone Expense			4 171 00	
Salaries Expense			241 380 00	
Payroll Tax Expense			13 104 00	
Supplies Expense			6 060 00	
Insurance Expense			5 000 00	
Depreciation Expense—Equipment			7 420 00	
Uncollectible Accounts Expense			2 600 00	
Total Operating Expenses				279 735 00
Income from Operations				60 651 00
Other Expenses				
Interest Expense				2 160 00
Net Income for Year				58 491 00

SOLUTION (continued)

(2.)

Sports Warehouse
Statement of Owner's Equity
Year Ended December 31, 2013

Raul Flores, Capital, Jan. 1, 2013		260,730.00
Net Income for Year	58,491.00	
Less Withdrawals for the Year	50,000.00	
Increase in Capital		8,491.00
Raul Flores, Capital, Dec. 31, 2013		269,221.00

(3.)

Sports Warehouse
Balance Sheet
December 31, 2013

Assets		
Current Assets		
Cash		24,285.00
Accounts Receivable	61,258.00	
Less Allowance for Doubtful Accounts	5,930.00	55,328.00
Merchandise Inventory		197,214.00
Prepaid Expenses		
Supplies	3,512.00	
Prepaid Insurance	37,000.00	40,512.00
Total Current Assets		317,339.00
Plant and Equipment		
Equipment	83,290.00	
Less Accumulated Depreciation	24,330.00	
Total Plant and Equipment		58,960.00
Total Assets		376,299.00
Liabilities and Owner's Equity		
Current Liabilities		
Notes Payable	47,500.00	
Accounts Payable	44,860.00	
Interest Payable	3,660.00	
Social Security Tax Payable	2,683.00	
Medicare Tax Payable	845.00	
Salaries Payable	7,530.00	
Total Current Liabilities		107,078.00
Owner's Equity		
Raul Flores, Capital		269,221.00
Total Liabilities and Owner's Equity		376,299.00

SOLUTION (continued)

(4.) GENERAL JOURNAL PAGE **45**

DATE		DESCRIPTION	POST. REF.	DEBIT	CREDIT
		Closing Entries			
2010					
Dec.	**31**	**Sales**		**625,690.00**	
		Purchase Returns and Allowances		**10,440.00**	
		Purchases Discounts		**11,921.00**	
		Income Summary			**648,051.00**
	31	**Income Summary**		**585,429.00**	
		Sales Returns and Allowances			**11,950.00**
		Purchases			**280,174.00**
		Freight In			**11,410.00**
		Telephone Expense			**4,171.00**
		Salaries Expense			**241,380.00**
		Payroll Taxes Expense			**13,104.00**
		Supplies Expense			**6,060.00**
		Insurance Expense			**5,000.00**
		Depreciation Expense—Equipment			**7,420.00**
		Uncollectible Accounts Expense			**2,600.00**
		Interest Expense			**2,160.00**
	31	**Income Summary**		**58,491.00**	
		Raul Flores, Capital			**58,491.00**
	31	**Raul Flores, Capital**		**50,000.00**	
		Raul Flores, Drawing			**50,000.00**

(5.) The gross profit percentage for the year ended December 31, 2013 is 55.5% ($340,386/$613,740).

(6.) The current ratio at December 31, 2013 is 2.96 ($317,339/$107,078).

(7.) The inventory turnover ratio for the year ended December 31, 2013 is 3.08 ($613,740/$199,279.50).

WORKING PAPERS

Name ______________________

EXERCISE 13.1

1. Purchases Returns and Allowances ____________
2. Telephone Expense ____________
3. Sales Returns and Allowances ____________
4. Purchases ____________
5. Interest Income ____________
6. Merchandise Inventory ____________
7. Interest Expense ____________
8. Sales ____________
9. Depreciation Expense—Store Equipment ____________
10. Rent Expense ____________

EXERCISE 13.2x

1. Accounts Receivable ____________
2. Delivery Van ____________
3. Prepaid Insurance ____________
4. Notes Payable, due 2014 ____________
5. Store Supplies ____________
6. Accounts Payable ____________
7. Merchandise Inventory ____________
8. Ray Lynch, Capital ____________
9. Cash ____________
10. Unearned Subscription Income ____________

EXERCISE 13.3

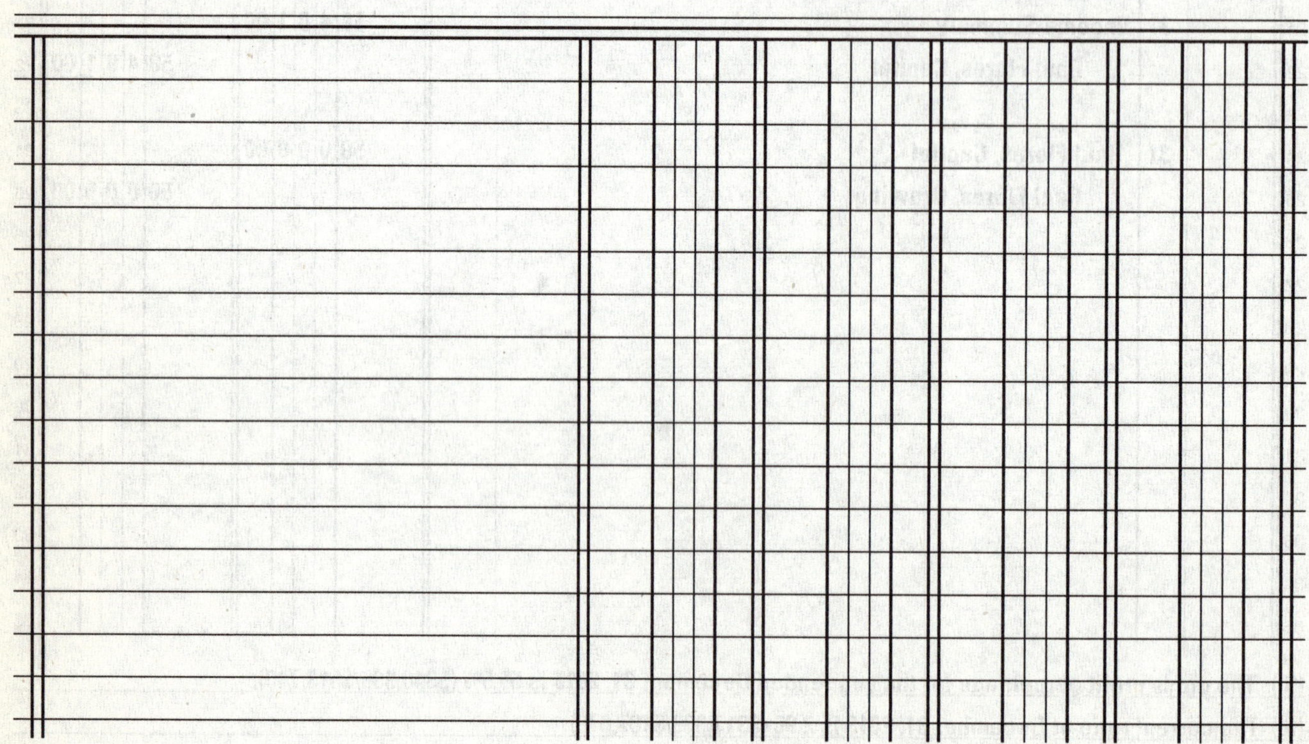

(continued)

Name

EXERCISE 13.3 (continued)

EXERCISE 13.4

Name

EXERCISE 13.5

Name ____________________

EXERCISE 13.6

GENERAL JOURNAL

PAGE ______

DATE		DESCRIPTION	POST. REF.	DEBIT	CREDIT

Name ______________________

EXERCISE 13.7

GENERAL JOURNAL

PAGE ________

DATE		DESCRIPTION	POST. REF.	DEBIT	CREDIT

Name

EXERCISE 13.8

ACCOUNT NAME	DEBIT	CREDIT

Name

EXERCISE 13.9

a. Net Sales is

Gross profit is

The gross profit percentage is

b. Current assets are

Current liabilities are

Working capital is

Name

EXERCISE 13.9 (continued)

c. The current ratio is

d. The inventory turnover is

Name ______________________

PROBLEM 13.1A or 13.1B

(continued)

Name

PROBLEM 13.1A or 13.1B (continued)

Name

PROBLEM 13.1A or 13.1B (continued)

(continued)

Name

PROBLEM 13.1A or 13.1B (continued)

Analyze:

Name

PROBLEM 13.2A or 13.2B

(continued)

Name

PROBLEM 13.2A or 13.2B (continued)

Name

PROBLEM 13.2A or 13.2B (continued)

(continued)

Name

PROBLEM 13.2A or 13.2B (continued)

Analyze:

Name

PROBLEM 13.3A or 13.3B

(continued)

Name

PROBLEM 13.3A or 13.3B (continued)

Name

PROBLEM 13.3A or 13.3B (continued)

(continued)

Name

PROBLEM 13.3A or 13.3B (continued)

Analyze:

Name ____________________

PROBLEM 13.4A or 13.4B

GENERAL JOURNAL

PAGE ______

DATE	DESCRIPTION	POST. REF.	DEBIT	CREDIT

Name

PROBLEM 13.4A or 13.4B (continued)

GENERAL JOURNAL

PAGE

DATE		DESCRIPTION	POST. REF.	DEBIT	CREDIT

Name

PROBLEM 13.4A or 13.4B (continued)

GENERAL JOURNAL

PAGE

DATE	DESCRIPTION	POST. REF.	DEBIT	CREDIT

Name

PROBLEM 13.4A or 13.4B (continued)

GENERAL JOURNAL

PAGE

DATE		DESCRIPTION	POST. REF.	DEBIT	CREDIT

Analyze:

PAGE

DATE		DESCRIPTION	POST. REF.	DEBIT	CREDIT

Name

PROBLEM 13.5A or 13.5B

GENERAL JOURNAL

PAGE

DATE		DESCRIPTION	POST. REF.	DEBIT	CREDIT

Name

PROBLEM 13.5A or 13.5B (continued)

GENERAL JOURNAL

PAGE

DATE	DESCRIPTION	POST. REF.	DEBIT	CREDIT

Analyze:

EXTRA FORM

GENERAL JOURNAL

PAGE

DATE	DESCRIPTION	POST. REF.	DEBIT	CREDIT

Name

CRITICAL THINKING PROBLEM 13.1

ACCOUNT NAME	TRIAL BALANCE		ADJUSTMENTS	
	DEBIT	CREDIT	DEBIT	CREDIT

Name

CRITICAL THINKING PROBLEM 13.1 (continued)

ADJUSTED TRIAL BALANCE		INCOME STATEMENT		BALANCE SHEET		
DEBIT	CREDIT	DEBIT	CREDIT	DEBIT	CREDIT	
						1
						2
						3
						4
						5
						6
						7
						8
						9
						10
						11
						12
						13
						14
						15
						16
						17
						18
						19
						20
						21
						22
						23
						24
						25
						26
						27
						28
						29
						30
						31
						32
						33
						34
						35
						36

Name

CRITICAL THINKING PROBLEM 13.1 (continued)

Name

CRITICAL THINKING PROBLEM 13.1 (continued)

EXTRA FORM

Name

CRITICAL THINKING PROBLEM 13.1 (continued)

Name

CRITICAL THINKING PROBLEM 13.1 (continued)

GENERAL JOURNAL

PAGE

DATE	DESCRIPTION	POST. REF.	DEBIT	CREDIT

Name

CRITICAL THINKING PROBLEM 13.1 (continued)

GENERAL JOURNAL PAGE

	DATE	DESCRIPTION	POST. REF.	DEBIT	CREDIT	
1						1
2						2
3						3
4						4
5						5
6						6
7						7
8						8
9						9
10						10
11						11
12						12
13						13
14						14
15						15
16						16
17						17
18						18
19						19
20						20
21						21
22						22
23						23
24						24
25						25
26						26
27						27
28						28
29						29
30						30
31						31
32						32
33						33
34						34
35						35
36						36
37						37

Name ____________________

CRITICAL THINKING PROBLEM 13.1 (continued)

GENERAL JOURNAL

PAGE ________

DATE	DESCRIPTION	POST. REF.	DEBIT	CREDIT

Name ______________________

CRITICAL THINKING PROBLEM 13.1 (continued)

GENERAL JOURNAL PAGE ________

	DATE	DESCRIPTION	POST. REF.	DEBIT	CREDIT	
1						1
2						2
3						3
4						4
5						5
6						6
7						7
8						8
9						9
10						10
11						11
12						12
13						13
14						14
15						15
16						16
17						17
18						18
19						19
20						20
21						21
22						22
23						23
24						24
25						25
26						26
27						27
28						28
29						29
30						30
31						31
32						32
33						33
34						34

Analyze: ______________________

Name

CRITICAL THINKING PROBLEM 13.2

1.

2.

Name

CHAPTER 13 CRITICAL THINKING PROBLEM (continued)

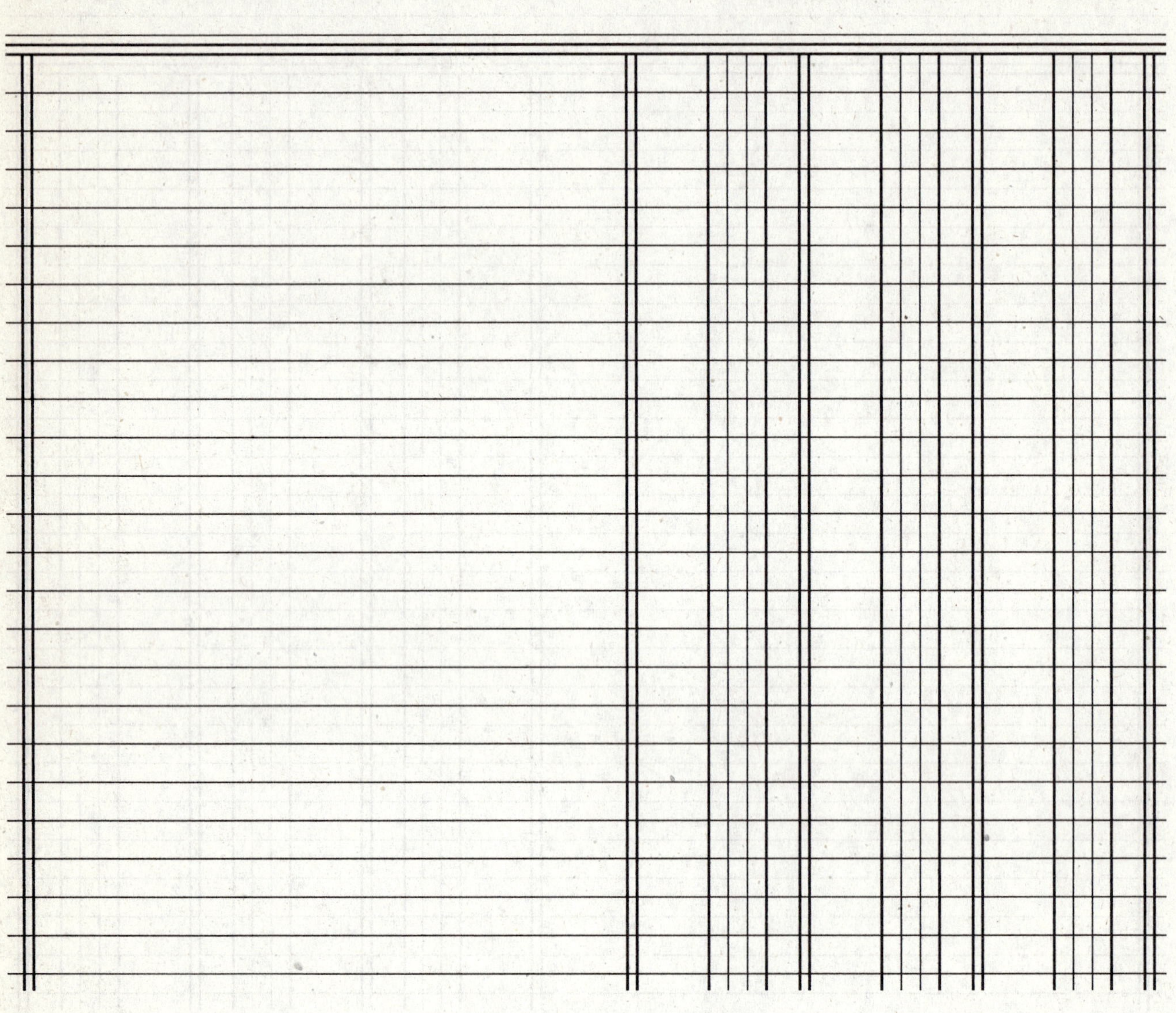

3.

Chapter 13 Practice Test Answer Key

Part A True-False

1. F	6. T	11. F	16. T	21. F
2. T	7. F	12. T	17. T	22. F
3. F	8. F	13. F	18. T	23. T
4. F	9. T	14. F	19. T	24. T
5. T	10. F	15. F	20. T	25. F

MINI-PRACTICE SET 2

Name ______________________

Merchandising Business Accounting Cycle

SALES JOURNAL

PAGE ______

DATE	SALES SLIP NO.	CUSTOMER'S NAME	POST. REF.	ACCOUNTS RECEIVABLE DEBIT	SALES TAX PAYABLE CREDIT	SALES CREDIT

PURCHASES JOURNAL

PAGE ______

DATE	PURCHASED FROM	INVOICE NUMBER	INVOICE DATE	TERMS	POST. REF.	PURCHASES DR./ ACCOUNTS PAYABLE CREDIT

 Name

CASH RECEIPTS JOURNAL

PAGE ______

DATE	DESCRIPTION	POST. REF.	ACCOUNTS RECEIVABLE CREDIT	SALES TAX PAYABLE CREDIT	SALES CREDIT	OTHER ACCOUNTS CREDIT			CASH DEBIT
						ACCOUNT NAME	POST. REF.	AMOUNT	

 Name ____________________

CASH PAYMENTS JOURNAL

PAGE ____

DATE	CK. NO.	DESCRIPTION	POST. REF.	ACCOUNTS PAYABLE DEBIT	OTHER ACCOUNTS DEBIT			PURCHASES DISCOUNTS CREDIT	CASH CREDIT
					ACCOUNT NAME	POST. REF.	AMOUNT		

 Name

GENERAL JOURNAL

PAGE

DATE		DESCRIPTION	POST. REF.	DEBIT	CREDIT

 Name ____________

GENERAL JOURNAL PAGE ______

DATE		DESCRIPTION	POST. REF.	DEBIT	CREDIT

MINI-PRACTICE SET 2 (continued)

Name ____________________

GENERAL JOURNAL

PAGE ________

DATE		DESCRIPTION	POST. REF.	DEBIT	CREDIT

 Name

GENERAL LEDGER

ACCOUNT ACCOUNT NO.

DATE		DESCRIPTION	POST. REF.	DEBIT	CREDIT	BALANCE	
						DEBIT	CREDIT

ACCOUNT ACCOUNT NO.

DATE		DESCRIPTION	POST. REF.	DEBIT	CREDIT	BALANCE	
						DEBIT	CREDIT

ACCOUNT ACCOUNT NO.

DATE		DESCRIPTION	POST. REF.	DEBIT	CREDIT	BALANCE	
						DEBIT	CREDIT

ACCOUNT ACCOUNT NO.

DATE		DESCRIPTION	POST. REF.	DEBIT	CREDIT	BALANCE	
						DEBIT	CREDIT

 Name

GENERAL LEDGER

ACCOUNT ACCOUNT NO.

DATE		DESCRIPTION	POST. REF.	DEBIT	CREDIT	BALANCE	
						DEBIT	CREDIT

ACCOUNT ACCOUNT NO.

DATE		DESCRIPTION	POST. REF.	DEBIT	CREDIT	BALANCE	
						DEBIT	CREDIT

ACCOUNT ACCOUNT NO.

DATE		DESCRIPTION	POST. REF.	DEBIT	CREDIT	BALANCE	
						DEBIT	CREDIT

ACCOUNT ACCOUNT NO.

DATE		DESCRIPTION	POST. REF.	DEBIT	CREDIT	BALANCE	
						DEBIT	CREDIT

ACCOUNT ACCOUNT NO.

DATE		DESCRIPTION	POST. REF.	DEBIT	CREDIT	BALANCE	
						DEBIT	CREDIT

 Name

GENERAL LEDGER

ACCOUNT ACCOUNT NO.

DATE		DESCRIPTION	POST. REF.	DEBIT	CREDIT	BALANCE	
						DEBIT	CREDIT

ACCOUNT ACCOUNT NO.

DATE		DESCRIPTION	POST. REF.	DEBIT	CREDIT	BALANCE	
						DEBIT	CREDIT

ACCOUNT ACCOUNT NO.

DATE		DESCRIPTION	POST. REF.	DEBIT	CREDIT	BALANCE	
						DEBIT	CREDIT

ACCOUNT ACCOUNT NO.

DATE		DESCRIPTION	POST. REF.	DEBIT	CREDIT	BALANCE	
						DEBIT	CREDIT

 Name

GENERAL LEDGER

ACCOUNT ACCOUNT NO.

DATE		DESCRIPTION	POST. REF.	DEBIT	CREDIT	BALANCE DEBIT	BALANCE CREDIT

ACCOUNT ACCOUNT NO.

DATE		DESCRIPTION	POST. REF.	DEBIT	CREDIT	BALANCE DEBIT	BALANCE CREDIT

ACCOUNT ACCOUNT NO.

DATE		DESCRIPTION	POST. REF.	DEBIT	CREDIT	BALANCE DEBIT	BALANCE CREDIT

ACCOUNT ACCOUNT NO.

DATE		DESCRIPTION	POST. REF.	DEBIT	CREDIT	BALANCE DEBIT	BALANCE CREDIT

ACCOUNT ACCOUNT NO.

DATE		DESCRIPTION	POST. REF.	DEBIT	CREDIT	BALANCE DEBIT	BALANCE CREDIT

 Name

GENERAL LEDGER

ACCOUNT ACCOUNT NO.

DATE		DESCRIPTION	POST. REF.	DEBIT	CREDIT	BALANCE	
						DEBIT	CREDIT

ACCOUNT ACCOUNT NO.

DATE		DESCRIPTION	POST. REF.	DEBIT	CREDIT	BALANCE	
						DEBIT	CREDIT

ACCOUNT ACCOUNT NO.

DATE		DESCRIPTION	POST. REF.	DEBIT	CREDIT	BALANCE	
						DEBIT	CREDIT

ACCOUNT ACCOUNT NO.

DATE		DESCRIPTION	POST. REF.	DEBIT	CREDIT	BALANCE	
						DEBIT	CREDIT

 Name

GENERAL LEDGER

ACCOUNT ACCOUNT NO.

DATE		DESCRIPTION	POST. REF.	DEBIT	CREDIT	BALANCE	
						DEBIT	CREDIT

ACCOUNT ACCOUNT NO.

DATE		DESCRIPTION	POST. REF.	DEBIT	CREDIT	BALANCE	
						DEBIT	CREDIT

ACCOUNT ACCOUNT NO.

DATE		DESCRIPTION	POST. REF.	DEBIT	CREDIT	BALANCE	
						DEBIT	CREDIT

ACCOUNT ACCOUNT NO.

DATE		DESCRIPTION	POST. REF.	DEBIT	CREDIT	BALANCE	
						DEBIT	CREDIT

ACCOUNT ACCOUNT NO.

DATE		DESCRIPTION	POST. REF.	DEBIT	CREDIT	BALANCE	
						DEBIT	CREDIT

 Name

GENERAL LEDGER

ACCOUNT ACCOUNT NO.

DATE		DESCRIPTION	POST. REF.	DEBIT	CREDIT	BALANCE DEBIT	BALANCE CREDIT

ACCOUNT ACCOUNT NO.

DATE		DESCRIPTION	POST. REF.	DEBIT	CREDIT	BALANCE DEBIT	BALANCE CREDIT

ACCOUNT ACCOUNT NO.

DATE		DESCRIPTION	POST. REF.	DEBIT	CREDIT	BALANCE DEBIT	BALANCE CREDIT

ACCOUNT ACCOUNT NO.

DATE		DESCRIPTION	POST. REF.	DEBIT	CREDIT	BALANCE DEBIT	BALANCE CREDIT

ACCOUNT ACCOUNT NO.

DATE		DESCRIPTION	POST. REF.	DEBIT	CREDIT	BALANCE DEBIT	BALANCE CREDIT

 Name

GENERAL LEDGER

ACCOUNT ACCOUNT NO.

DATE		DESCRIPTION	POST. REF.	DEBIT	CREDIT	BALANCE	
						DEBIT	CREDIT

ACCOUNT ACCOUNT NO.

DATE		DESCRIPTION	POST. REF.	DEBIT	CREDIT	BALANCE	
						DEBIT	CREDIT

ACCOUNT ACCOUNT NO.

DATE		DESCRIPTION	POST. REF.	DEBIT	CREDIT	BALANCE	
						DEBIT	CREDIT

ACCOUNT ACCOUNT NO.

DATE		DESCRIPTION	POST. REF.	DEBIT	CREDIT	BALANCE	
						DEBIT	CREDIT

ACCOUNT ACCOUNT NO.

DATE		DESCRIPTION	POST. REF.	DEBIT	CREDIT	BALANCE	
						DEBIT	CREDIT

 Name ______

ACCOUNTS RECEIVABLE SUBSIDIARY LEDGER

NAME ______ TERMS ______

DATE		DESCRIPTION	POST. REF.	DEBIT	CREDIT	BALANCE

NAME ______ TERMS ______

DATE		DESCRIPTION	POST. REF.	DEBIT	CREDIT	BALANCE

NAME ______ TERMS ______

DATE		DESCRIPTION	POST. REF.	DEBIT	CREDIT	BALANCE

NAME ______ TERMS ______

DATE		DESCRIPTION	POST. REF.	DEBIT	CREDIT	BALANCE

NAME ______ TERMS ______

DATE		DESCRIPTION	POST. REF.	DEBIT	CREDIT	BALANCE

 Name

ACCOUNTS RECEIVABLE SUBSIDIARY LEDGER

NAME TERMS

DATE		DESCRIPTION	POST. REF.	DEBIT	CREDIT	BALANCE

NAME TERMS

DATE		DESCRIPTION	POST. REF.	DEBIT	CREDIT	BALANCE

ACCOUNTS PAYABLE SUBSIDIARY LEDGER

NAME TERMS

DATE		DESCRIPTION	POST. REF.	DEBIT	CREDIT	BALANCE

NAME TERMS

DATE		DESCRIPTION	POST. REF.	DEBIT	CREDIT	BALANCE

 Name

ACCOUNTS PAYABLE SUBSIDIARY LEDGER

NAME ______________________ TERMS ______

DATE		DESCRIPTION	POST. REF.	DEBIT	CREDIT	BALANCE

 Name ____________________

	ACCOUNT NAME	TRIAL BALANCE		ADJUSTMENTS	
		DEBIT	CREDIT	DEBIT	CREDIT
1					
2					
3					
4					
5					
6					
7					
8					
9					
10					
11					
12					
13					
14					
15					
16					
17					
18					
19					
20					
21					
22					
23					
24					
25					
26					
27					
28					
29					
30					
31					
32					
33					
34					
35					
36					

MINI-PRACTICE SET 2 (continued)

Name ______________________

ADJUSTED TRIAL BALANCE		INCOME STATEMENT		BALANCE SHEET		
DEBIT	CREDIT	DEBIT	CREDIT	DEBIT	CREDIT	
						1
						2
						3
						4
						5
						6
						7
						8
						9
						10
						11
						12
						13
						14
						15
						16
						17
						18
						19
						20
						21
						22
						23
						24
						25
						26
						27
						28
						29
						30
						31
						32
						33
						34
						35
						36

Name

ACCOUNT NAME	TRIAL BALANCE		ADJUSTMENTS	
	DEBIT	CREDIT	DEBIT	CREDIT

 Name ______________________

ADJUSTED TRIAL BALANCE		INCOME STATEMENT		BALANCE SHEET		
DEBIT	CREDIT	DEBIT	CREDIT	DEBIT	CREDIT	
						1
						2
						3
						4
						5
						6
						7
						8
						9
						10
						11
						12
						13
						14
						15
						16
						17
						18
						19
						20
						21
						22
						23
						24
						25
						26
						27
						28
						29
						30
						31
						32
						33
						34
						35
						36

Name ______________________

Name

Name

Name

ACCOUNT NAME	DEBIT	CREDIT

 Name ____________________

EXTRA FORMS

	ACCOUNT NAME	TRIAL BALANCE		ADJUSTMENTS	
		DEBIT	CREDIT	DEBIT	CREDIT
1					
2					
3					
4					
5					
6					
7					
8					
9					
10					
11					
12					
13					
14					
15					
16					
17					
18					
19					
20					
21					
22					
23					
24					
25					
26					
27					
28					
29					
30					
31					
32					
33					
34					

MINI-PRACTICE SET 2 (continued)

Name ____________________

ADJUSTED TRIAL BALANCE		INCOME STATEMENT		BALANCE SHEET	
DEBIT	CREDIT	DEBIT	CREDIT	DEBIT	CREDIT

Name ____________________

EXTRA FORM

GENERAL JOURNAL

PAGE ________

DATE	DESCRIPTION	POST. REF.	DEBIT	CREDIT